ISBN 978-1-331-23981-9
PIBN 10162924

1 MONTH OF
FREE
READING

at
www.ForgottenBooks.com

By purchasing this book you are eligible for one month membership to ForgottenBooks.com, giving you unlimited access to our entire collection of over 700,000 titles via our web site and mobile apps.

To claim your free month visit:

www.forgottenbooks.com/free162924

English
Français
Deutsche
Italiano
Español
Português

www.forgottenbooks.com

Mythology Photography **Fiction**
Fishing Christianity **Art** Cooking
Essays Buddhism Freemasonry
Medicine **Biology** Music **Ancient
Egypt** Evolution Carpentry Physics
Dance Geology **Mathematics** Fitness
Shakespeare **Folklore** Yoga Marketing
Confidence Immortality Biographies
Poetry **Psychology** Witchcraft
Electronics Chemistry History **Law**
Accounting **Philosophy** Anthropology
Alchemy Drama Quantum Mechanics
Atheism Sexual Health **Ancient History**
Entrepreneurship Languages Sport
Paleontology Needlework Islam
Metaphysics Investment Archaeology
Parenting Statistics Criminology
Motivational

BY

WILLIAM ALEXANDER MaCCORKLE, LL.D.

LATE GOVERNOR OF WEST VIRGINIA

———

G. P. PUTNAM'S SONS

NEW YORK AND LONDON

The Knickerbocker Press

1908

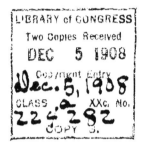

COPYRIGHT, 1908
BY
WILLIAM ALEXANDER MacCORKLE

The Knickerbocker Press, New York

TO

JOSEPH E. CHILTON AND WILLIAM E. CHILTON

MY PARTNERS AND THE FRIENDS OF MANY YEARS

THIS BOOK IS AFFECTIONATELY INSCRIBED

PREFACE

THIS book is composed of six addresses, delivered at various times and places, on questions in which the South is interested.

The first address discusses *The Negro and the Intelligence and Property Franchise*, and was delivered before the Southern Conference of Race Problems at Montgomery, Alabama, May 9, 1900.

The second deals with *Some Phases of the Race Question*, and was delivered before the Southern Industrial Convention at Huntsville, Alabama, October, 12, 1899.

The third considers *The Attitude of the Progressive South*, and was delivered at the Annual Dinner of the Board of Trade of Newark, New Jersey, January 18, 1900.

The fourth considers *The Experience of this Republic as to the Elective Franchise*, and was delivered before the Nineteenth Century Club in New York City, January 15, 1901.

The fifth discusses *Some Tendencies of the Day*, and was delivered before the Societies of Roanoke College, Salem, Virginia, June 10, 1902.

The sixth is a discussion of *The Patriotism of the South in Reference to the Conditions of the Times*. The last was delivered at the Commencement of Washington and Lee University at Lexington, Virginia, on June 17, 1908.

As will be seen the addresses were intended for the platform and they are printed just as they were delivered, with no change of verbiage or sentiment.

I can give no excuses for publishing them, beyond the hope that in some small degree they might assist in the settlement of the grave questions confronting the South.

CHARLESTON, WEST VIRGINIA,
    July 25, 1908.

CONTENTS

I

THE NEGRO AND THE INTELLIGENCE AND PROPERTY FRANCHISES

BY the overkind appreciation of the Chairman of the Committee, I am asked to conclude the debate on this great question, which has within it such potentialities for good or evil to this land, resting under the splendor of the May-day sunshine, a land from whose kingly plenitude of moral and material worth man can reap more abundantly and more easily than at any time since, by the Divine command, fruition was crowned with the toil of the hands.

Coming from the mountains of West Virginia, within the sound of the flow of the Beautiful River, yet I am no stranger to Alabama or to her traditions and her glory ; and when, inclining her proud head to the inscrutable commands of the Great Ruler of governments and armies, she pressed to her pure lips in the day of her agony and sorrow the cup filled with the bitter waters of Marah, I and mine, from the same chalice of suffering, drank the consuming draught of humiliation and distress.

Some Southern Questions

This fair city, pulsating with busy life, hallowed with memories of the past, laden to-day with the sweet luxuriance and redolency of springtime flowers typical of that resurrection which will not wither with the passing of their fragrance, where amidst your foliage-embowered streets I seem to hear the thunderous tread of a mighty spirit, is to me the Mecca of a pilgrimage which I approach with bared head and unsandaled feet. Holding views as to this great question under discussion differing somewhat from those of the distinguished and honored sons of the South who have preceded me, yet I yield to them nothing, not a hand's breadth, in love for the South, reverence for her glorious past, and glowing hope for the sure consummation of her splendid destiny.

Seeing first the light of day and passing the springtime of life in the town where sleep, under the soft shadows of our mountains, Lee and Jackson, words untrue to the South uttered on this classic scene would blister the tongue of him who gave them birth. Every tradition of my people, their joys, their sorrows, and their loves, have their resting-place on the spotless and consecrated bosom of old Virginia, and my every hope and ambition for the future is intertwined in the welfare and good of the South. The limpid sunlight of the South and the azure of her sky hold me in a spell which appeals to my soul with a witchery far more potent than happier material conditions amidst other associations and surrounded by other peoples. For her sake, the old home, fragrant with precious and unspeakable memories of the smile around the hearth and rich with the sunlight of the gentle voices in the wide halls in other and happier days, echoes to the footsteps of the alien master ; and our fields, under the Divine ordering of Him who, with impartial hand, distils the dew and scatters the sunshine, yield their treasures of rich grain to the hand of the stranger. For her sake, without repining, I have sat at the widow's board, where the barrel of meal wasted and the cruse of oil failed ; and whilst differing on this question with possibly a majority of the audience before me, yet in the sweet words of affection, old as the love which crowned with glory of surpassing light the tall pines on the lonely mountains of Moab and gladdened the ripening grain in the harvest-fields of Judea, " Entreat me not to leave thee or return from following after thee, for whither thou goest I will go, and where thou lodgest I will lodge."

Appreciating the importance of this great question to our country, and well recognizing my poverty of experience and ability, I approach the discussion with that diffidence born of a desire that no spirit except the love of my country shall guide my statements and direct my thoughts. On the threshold I pray to the good God of our people that we may reason with each other in a spirit of calmness which will lead us to that high plane where we can put away all feelings less holy than the love of country, and from the sublime heights of true patriotism look down on every unworthy ambition.

The settlement of the Race Question, in the present

acute condition of the public mind, will take its true direction within the next few years; and the South deserves to have the true expression and the honest action of her sons, unclouded and unbiased by personal ambition or untrammelled by partisan command. Never before did modern civilization have such deep and abiding interest in the ultimate action of a portion of its elements as it has now in the action of the people of the South. Here, I pray and believe, will be witnessed the sublimest consummation of true statesmanship and realization of popular government by a people, who, though prejudiced by local conditions, hampered by another and alien race, and vexed by social and economic conditions such as never before beset a people, yet rising above the complications of the hour, are honestly, impartially, without prejudice, and with full justice solving this question to the glory of the whole people. Surely, it will take all of our strength to close rightly the only question which has kept apart the people of this mighty Republic, and which has given anxious thought to those who look towards our land for the blessed realization of a government by the people. Only in a spirit of compromise, as exemplified by the Fathers, who gave up cherished convictions that all might meet on a plane on which a government could be inaugurated and successfully conducted, can we to-day succeed. " And thus the Constitution which we now present, is the result of a spirit of amity and of that mutual deference and concession which the peculi-

arity of our political situation rendered indispensable."
The obeisance which we owe the glorious traditions of
our past, and the commanding position of the South in
this marvellous and splendid cycle of material development, demand that sobriety of action, tolerance of
spirit, and charity of opinion which has ever characterized a free people in the solving of the great questions
which meet every people designed by Providence for a
permanent place among the nations.   Says Mr. Hume:

"There are enough of zealots on both sides who
kindle up the passions of their partisans, and, under
the pretence of public good, pursue the interest and
ends of their particular faction.   For my part, I shall
always be more fond of promoting moderation than
zeal; though perhaps the surest way of producing moderation in every party is to increase our zeal for the
public.   Let us therefore try, if it be possible, from the
foregoing to draw a lesson of moderation with regard to
the parties into which our country is at present divided;
at the same time, that we allow not this moderation to
abate the industry and passion with which every individual is bound to pursue the good of his country."

In the solution of this great problem, surely we can
rise above the heat of political discussion, and show to
the world complete abnegation of previously formed
opinion, and allow our spirits to be touched by that
charity which comes alone from Him who, amidst the
complexities of change and despair of our future, has
always guided us in those ways best for His people.

I shall not attempt to discuss the minor and infinitely varied details of this important question. I shall rather briefly, and in my humble way, found my argument upon the basic principles of our national existence, and upon some general principles, and not waste your time in assaulting the outworks of the citadel.

The settlement of this franchise question lies deep upon the very foundation-stones of the Republic, and only by laying bare to the people's view those mighty substructures can we here efficiently serve our country.

Every historic state is underlaid with a fundamental principle, from which it breathes its life and through which it has its civil existence. Each of our colonies had its peculiar idea of government; but after they were bound in one glorious, shining union of States, that great principle of civil philosophy, the right of the people to govern through its own suffrage, shone as the glory of heaven. The State became the sovereign through the power of its own people, and the preservation of its liberty was predicated upon the people.

Therefore, I assert that the constitutional exercise of the right of franchise is the vital and underlying principle of the life of this free people, and that the infraction of this principle is surely attended with ultimate ruin to our system of republican government. " In democracy, there can be no exercise of sovereignty but by the suffrages of the people which are their will."

Sir, this is fundamental, and, in this splendid presence, it but needs expression to receive assent. Stripped of every covering, it is but the annunciation of the right of the people to choose their servants, indicate their policy, and live under the laws they themselves have created. When you depart from this principle, you forsake the underlying principle of national government; and when this is done, surely you drop out of the nations which exercise an abiding power upon civilization.

To enable our country to consummate its destiny, this vital principle, at the risk of weariness of expression, must be kept close to the hearts of the people. It is the golden thread, which at every stage of our national existence, through storm and battle and change, has been held by the patriots to inhere into the very texture of national life. When this principle is abandoned or impaired,

> " Our own
> Like free states foregone, is but a bright leaf torn
> From Time's dark forest, and on the wide gust thrown
> To float awhile, by varying eddies borne;
> And sink at last forever!"

Says Montesquieu: "It is plain, then, that if the government, whether State or Federal, controls or disposes of suffrage, or allows it to be disposed of, without warrant in the Constitution, it strikes at the very vitals of the republic from which it derives its entire existence and power."

In all the ages, the ruin of free nations has been wrought through the insidious sapping and impairing

of the fundamental principle vitalizing the government. I appeal to the historic past as the unerring
guide to the future. I am reminded that the power
of the Great Republic stretches this year into two
hemispheres; that in ships and money and all of the
elements of power and grandeur and civilization since
the morning stars sang together she has not had her
equal. Permit me, sir, to recall to you that the real
impairment of the integrity of the governing principle
of every historic state dated from the brightest splendor
of its existence and not from the hour of its weakness.
I call from the solemn past the phantom memories of
Greece and Judea and kingly Rome. When the silks
and purple and fine linen of Tyre and Sidon were in
every market-place, and the light of the star of the
Blessed Redeemer was already touching with its holy
fires the lofty towers of the Temple of the Living
Jehovah, Judea was stricken. When the genius of
Socrates, Plato, Aristotle, Demosthenes, and Euripides
held in mortal thrall the intelligence of the world, and
the statue of Pallas Athenæ and the columned Parthenon looked down on the Piræus, filled with the
ships from the Euxine, the Ægean, and from beyond
the Pillars of Hercules, and when the glory from Sala-
mis and Thermopylæ thrilled the people and lighted
up the beacons of Democracy on Naxos and Delos and
the Islands of the Sea, Greece was stricken. When
her arms extended from Dacia to the Desert of Libya,
and the thunderous tread of her legions shook the

known world, and her mariners plucked the fruit from the mystic Garden of the Hesperides, and the oar-beat of her triremes shook the mist of the Hyperborean Seas, and Gaul and Scythian and Christian appealed to her royal power, Rome was stricken.

But, sir, the student of the philosophy of government points to the important distinction that Rome and Greece were guarded by the genius of the philosophers, and Judea by the patriarchs, the prophets, and the lawgivers, but that neither Greece nor Rome nor Judea was illumined by the Master, upon whose teachings are founded the principles of the modern state. In reply, sir, Holland, a modern state, is an illustration of the immutable rule that, whether under the teachings of the brows encircled by the chaplet of ivy and laurel or by the Crown of Thorns, the basic principle of civil life controlling the state cannot be impaired without ultimate ruin. Under the inspiration of religion, uplifted by the genius of freedom, grasping the great principle of representative union of Hansetown and Provence, defying Spain, establishing her colonies in all the earth, bidding fair to become a great, abiding, historic people and divide with England the control of the commercial and civilizing influences of the world, Holland, intoxicated with power, forgot the basic principle which made her great, and sank to the rank of a lesser national power having no future historic importance.

Then, sir, reasoning from the past, with all the

intensity of my life, I plead for the maintenance, in its original integrity, of the underlying principle of our Republic. It is supremely vital to liberty. Dethrone the principle from its high estate, and the temple of Liberty is already tottering. Political apostasy is terrible in its reach and grasp of power and in the quick emulation of its example. The infraction of the right of franchise, the impairment of the constitutional right of the citizen to exercise the franchise in South Carolina or in Alabama, provoke the desire and willingness to commit the same wrong in the populous city of New York or in Pennsylvania. The passing of enactments at Montgomery or Charleston, interfering with and restricting the franchise against the spirit of the Constitution and its amendments, provokes the terror of the Force Bill in the National House and Senate. The impairment of the constitutional right in the States causes equal emulation for the destruction of our constitutional guarantees by laying the hand of political apostasy upon the Constitution of the United States.

"Familiarize yourself with the chains of bondage and you prepare your own limbs to wear them. Accustomed to trample on the rights of others, you have lost the strength of your own independence and become the fit subjects of the first cunning tyrant who rises among you."

Men desiring to grasp unconstitutional power heed little the cry of a people that any infraction of that

great instrument by them was caused by the overweening necessity of preserving their civilization from destruction. At this transition period of the world's
history, the conservative forces of the country should
be on their guard to save the Republic from any impairment of its fundamental principles. The times are
surely propitious for such injury to our governing principle, and the example of its infraction too recent to
brook denial. The growth of the sentiment that the
Constitution is what the majority of the people wish it
to be, the growing power of wealth and class in the
elections, the increasing control of the central government and its gradual infringement upon the rights of
the States, the overweening power of the Federal Courts
upon every pretext seeking to control State tribunals
and exercise jurisdiction never contemplated by the
Constitution, the lessening respect for the elective franchise, and the want of regard for the dignity of the
States, sadly illustrated to-day by the warring governments of a free commonwealth, all show the vital
demand for the jealous care of the Constitution in all
of its original vigor.

Now, sir, the Fifteenth Amendment to the Constitution, "That the right of the citizens of the United
States to vote shall not be denied or abridged by the
United States or by any state on account of race, color,
or previous condition of servitude," is as much a part
and parcel of the organic law governing this country
as any section of the Constitution. Whether wisely or

not this amendment was ratified, I will not discuss, but under its provisions the Negro has with you and me an equal right to exercise the franchise. If we are an honest and constitution-loving people, we will give him his constitutional right. His privilege of franchise is as sacred as ours, and should be as sacredly guarded. This is the only principle which should animate the life of a free republic and upon which its continued existence can be predicated. I challenge any transgression whatsoever without ultimate and grievous hurt to the Constitution, and as grave injury to the white man as to the black. It is, I repeat and urge, the most sacred and solemn principle of the Constitution. With whatever earnestness I may have, I "declare that this ark of our political covenant, this Constitutional casket of our Confederated Nation, encasing as it does more of human liberty and human security and human life than any government ever founded by man, I would not break for the whole African race."

If we have, under the trying exigencies of the days of Reconstruction and new citizenship, wandered away from the spirit of the Constitution, let us ascend the mountains where we can see the tables of the law. Here, in this sacred city, consecrated with the life and blood and treasure of our people to the Constitution of our Fathers, I call upon our people to gather again within its majestic portals and hear the law and give full heed to its commands.

There can be but one response upon this question

from those who have communed in the sacred temple of the Constitution with the mighty beings who builded the sacred edifice. I answer for them that this question cannot be settled until it is settled right. I base my statement upon the eternal foundation of historic precedent and universal experience. I appeal to the facts of our own history which culminated in this city in the great drama which fiercely rocked the walls of civilization. I appeal for my argument to one higher than Cæsar. The deepening and broadening sense of eternal justice in the human heart decreed that slavery was wrong. The institution was surrounded by powers which never before girdled a civil institution. It was held in the letter of the law. It was hedged about by a patriotism unquestioned. It was jealously protected by the party which for sixty years had fought the battles of the Republic and which had added to it an imperial domain and which was deeply intrenched in the affections of the people. It was supported by the most supremely equipped statesmen who ever dazzled the world by the power of human intellect and statecraft. It was settled as the law of the land, by the binding decisions of the highest courts from whose decrees there was no appeal except to the supreme forum of the human heart. At the sacred birth of States, around whose bedsides sat the armed and panoplied and watchful hosts of the institution, it was settled. By solemn compromise of North and South, sealed by the House and Senate, by friend and foe, it was settled. By every human relation it was settled. Men walked in apparent security. Yet, sir, in that greatest forum under God, the eternal, immutable, unchangeable forum of human right, it was not settled. Before its bar the decrees of the highest earthly tribunal were dissipated as the morning dew. In the splendor of its court solemn enactment of Legislature and Senate and State was devoured as by consuming flames. Under its fiery ordeal compromise of statesmen shrivelled to ashes. It was not settled right; and not until decree of court and act of law and compromise of statesmen were deluged in blood, was it settled. I speak with no unkindness but with unspeakable tenderness of the memories of other days; and not for your imperial State, with its fields and flowing rivers and glowing furnaces, would I say aught unkind of the motives of the men who gave their sacred lives for what they believed was right. It illustrates, beyond the power of my tongue of weakness, that which I am striving to accentuate, that no question can be settled by a free people until it is settled in the forum of eternal justice. So I insist that until this question is settled right and in strict accord with the letter and spirit of the Constitution it will disturb our political relations, hold apart the North and South, hamper our development, degrade our civil liberty, pollute our franchise, endanger our freedom, and pillory us before the world as a people who do not do full and exact justice.

Sir, I beg that you will not understand for a moment

that these words are a concession that the real letter of the Constitution has been carelessly and wantonly violated by the South. I deny this charge with all my soul. I spurn with unspeakable contempt the reports of the frauds, violence, and intimidation with which the enemies of the South asperse her fair name. Her glory and her honor are to me as dear as life. Lay the book of nations wide open, and in all of the days there is none which through temptation and humiliation and sorrow has walked so steadily along the road of good government as has the South. Goaded with the bayonet, hedged about with the soldier, hounded by the alien, despoiled by the robber, her statehood decrowned and deflowered, since the morning of the world show me a country which emerged from suffering with garments as spotless and with so little of the smell of the fire about her. Yet, sir, while rejecting with disdain the calumnies against the South, still the time is upon us when we should commune with each other in a spirit of absolute fairness and most outspoken candor. It would be false to the spirit of truth pervading this Conference for me to deny that the South, appealing to a higher law than the Constitution or the statute, has never intended that the Negro should rule, or largely participate in the rule of her broad States and shape the destiny of her civilization. The time is here for plainness of speech, and he who would palter with the truth on this great question in its present portentous shape loves not his country. It is our duty to stand before the world and not swerve from the open light of discussion. If such has not been the intention of the South, then we are asked why this State Constitution provides the rule of understanding to be interpreted by the ballot commissioner as he may wish? Why this Constitution has inserted in it the ancestral clause? Why this Constitution provides a complicated election machinery? When you answer these insistent questions, your only reply can be that the great paramount reason for such action has been to preserve the State in the rule of the intelligent. With this reply there arises before us a broken and impaired Constitution, which has unloosed from its Pandora's box the foul vultures of coming woe, which are always ready to flap their wings about the dying body of a free people. It is from this anomalous condition of political affairs that the South must be released; and every Southern man, without regard to his political future, should rise to that height of love for country, where, caring not for the clamor of the hour, despising present utilitarianism, he can contemplate a country unbroken in its love, rich in material glory and domestic peace, over whose happy, contented, and united people is the shadow of a Constitution which, under the mercy of God, needs not to be broken to serve the higher law. If there be any faint-hearted and who would shrink, I would remind him that the day is surely propitious for the coming change; that there is upon the South one of those great cycles where

" All are raised and borne
By that great current in its onward sweep,
Wandering and rippling with caressing waves
Around green islands with the breath
Of flowers that never wither."

This cycle of industrial glory and regeneration, broadening like a golden river through the South, is assisting, with resistless power, the coming change. When the South was practically stationary in its development, when the planter waited for the rain to distil its drops into the cotton and the grain to imprison the gold of the sunshine, political anomalies, comparatively speaking, were unimportant. To-day the old South is being resurrected in a new form and exceeding glory. New peoples are clasping our hands, and, as bone of our bone, we are bidding them welcome to the dear land. Millions of dollars start the music of the machine and the engine. Mills are distilling their cloudy incense over our increasing fields. New cities lift their towering walls to the glory of our prosperity. Golden genii rise from the dark mines of the earth and hold out to us their offerings of commercial greatness. Our waterfalls are enthralled to add to our fulness, and the unerring winds of modern commerce have filled our harbors with the ships of the world.

The first demand of this industrial regeneration is the absolute settlement of political complexities. Its demand is even now insistent and we cannot, if we would, longer deny its potential request. The State which does so delay will not march abreast with its fellows in the industrial progress. This demand is as absolute and certain as any condition which ever touched a commercial and industrial existence. Then arises the crucial question, how can we remove our political complexities, give the Negro his franchise, and preserve the Constitution and at the same time not imperil our civilization? I reply that it seems to me by far the best to adopt an honest and inflexible educational and property basis administered fairly for black and white. By this method the white race controls the States he has created, and this control is based upon the eternal foundations of the law and the Constitution.

I crave your indulgence for a short time whilst I discuss this idea of an educational and property franchise, not in any detail, but in some of its higher and more general aspects. It appeals to the elements most needed in good citizenship. It will cultivate the desire for the acquisition of property and of education; and whilst attaining these two great ends of good government it will accomplish the immediate purpose for which we are striving, the settling and composing of our anomalous system of franchise. All of us hail the day of highest intelligence in those who control the government. Ignorance is the bottom of our woe. With the Negro made intelligent he is no longer dangerous to the State. He is no longer prey to the demagogue. With this system walks education with its uplifting and splendid effect upon the people. It is a necessary and vitalizing concomitant of the restricted franchise. This plan will not destroy the so essential self-respect of the Negro. It will allow him, through the open door, to see the play of the brightest light which touches the brow of any man, the splendid sun of American citizenship. He can grasp it, if he wishes it, without delay or wrong. It is his if he complies with the law, whose equal and fair provisions compel him to be a better citizen of his country, and a more intelligent and potent factor in his place. I believe that it would be an incentive to the acquisition of intelligence which could be attained so quickly in no other manner. He will no longer be the mere flotsam and jetsam of politics. My experience of political affairs is that as the Negro becomes intelligent so surely does he become a higher voting element, owing allegiance to no party as a mere matter of course. More than this, the adoption of this plan will bring to the South a fair, quick, and honest trial of the question of the Negro franchise. It will bring it in a manner which will cause no apprehension in the minds of any fair citizen. The question of Negro franchise has never yet been fairly tried. Let us a moment discuss this question. It is most important. The objection has been strenuously made against the adoption of a fair franchise system that we cannot safely proceed in the change. Is this a fair objection? I reiterate, sir, that it is not. Will the civilization of the South be affected

or impaired? Will the Negro vote overwhelm that of
the white? Is there necessity for the appeal to the
law of the Higher Defence? An investigation of the
status of the franchise shows that after the adoption
of an intelligence and property basis the political control of the South will be entirely under the domination
of the white man. A fair intelligence basis will practically produce the same result. An intelligence and property basis will give numerical control to the white man
entirely in every State, congressional district, and, with
only few exceptions, in every county in the South. There
is no shadow of suspicion that this fair franchise amendment will again give the Negroes control of the South.
Day by day, even the spectre of such contention dis-
appears before the industrial growth of the South.
Within the last few years from every country is seen
the line of immigration into the South. Along our
roads, in the streets of our cities, over our once quiet
fields, is heard the tramp of the thousands of feet of
those coming amongst us for the occupation of their
lives. Further, the white man is increasing in a far
greater ratio than the Negro. Aye, sir, we appeal to
the populations as they stand to-day, and, with all of the
earnestness demanded by the importance of the question, I ask, how can ten millions of comparatively ignorant Negroes overwhelm the civilization of twenty
millions of white people with the intelligence of all
the centuries behind them? Let us be fair, Mr. Chairman. Let us look the facts squarely in the face, and

not listen to our prejudices and our fears without foundation for either. I am reminded that we have once drunk of a bitter cup; that we have tried the Negro franchise; that upon the consideration of a fair franchise there arises before us the horrid phantasmagoria of the Reconstruction. Sir, every intelligent man, submitting himself to the calm, cold light of reason, must admit the absolute change of circumstances between then and now. There is no need for argument on this proposition. Consider yourself the status of affairs at that day, and you must admit that the Negro franchise was not fairly tried. The South prostrated, the boom of the cannon yet reverberating over the land, passions inflamed, men yet wearing the blue and the gray, the sword not yet turned into the scythe and the pruning-hook, the fields unploughed except by the furrow of war, your State government in the hands of your then enemy, your citizens disfranchised, with bound hands, standing about the ruins of their homes, the Negro only five years out of slavery and a citizen, I ask you, Mr. Chairman, in all fairness, are not the conditions changed as no conditions have ever been changed in any country within that period of time? Under this impartial view, I earnestly urge that no fair-minded man can say that a fair franchise in the South will bring back the days of Negro rule or the horrors of Reconstruction.

A careful investigation of the figures by Mr. Gannet,

a most careful and able expert, fully maintains my contention.   Let us appeal to the figures.

The three States of the South in which the Negro element is in greatest strength are South Carolina, Mississippi, and Louisiana.   If, by restricting suffrage in these States to the literate or to the property holders, or to the literate and the property holders, it would leave the whites in numerical majority, such restriction in other States would certainly have similar effect.

First, then, as to the matter of property holding.   I find that the owners of farms and homes in the three States in question are as follows :

FARMS AND HOMES.

Louisiana—

White owners	48,660
Colored owners	14,602

Mississippi—

White owners	61,500
Colored owners	16,956

South Carolina—

White owners	42,982
Colored owners	21,101

From the above, it is seen that, if the suffrage were restricted to those owning their farms or homes, the whites of South Carolina would outnumber the colored two to one ; of Mississippi, nearly four to one ; and of Louisiana, three and one-half to one.

The next question is on the matter of illiteracy, and here I present the following table, showing the total males and the illiterates over twenty years of age :

SOUTH CAROLINA.

	Whites.	Colored.
Males over 20 . .	106,665	139,479
Illiterate . .	15,814	91,387
Literate . .	90,851	48,092

MISSISSIPPI.

	Whites.	Colored.
Males over 20 . .	125,457	157,202
Illiterate . .	13,932	106,463
Literate . .	111,525	50,739

LOUISIANA.

	Whites.	Colored.
Males over 20 . .	136,106	125,194
Illiterate . .	24,161	90,487
Literate . .	111,945	34,707

Here we see that, if the suffrage be restricted to the literate, the whites of South Carolina would outnumber the colored nearly two to one ; those of Mississippi, more than two to one ; and those of Louisiana, more than three to one.

It must be remembered that these figures represent

the situation as it existed ten years ago. Doubtless, the Negroes have gained upon the whites in literacy to some extent during the decade, but certainly not sufficiently to change the general result.

In the light of these figures, can the argument of fear of Negro domination be sustained?

It is true that our first duty is the preservation of the civilization of the South upon the lines of our race, and this franchise provision does so upon the firm basis of justice and fairness. Then, sir, should we remain longer chained to the past?

Let us consider a most practical and potent reason why, as soon as possible, this or some other plan of settlement should be adopted which will hurry the Negro along the road of intelligent and settled citizenship. In this day of industrial and financial change, the South, in the adjustment of the commercial affairs in the next twenty-five years, will be the chief factor. We can no longer devote ourselves to the one and sole idea of holding ourselves solid on the Negro Question. Believing in the Southern leaders and trusting to their guidance in the past, still with the most absolute earnestness I believe that the time for change is upon us. The South has other things to occupy its attention. The great objection to the present system is that it demands our absolute attention and effectiveness to the exclusion of all else. We are busy. We are growing rich. We are the seat of a great commerce. Wealth is coming among us. This demands that we should have freedom of action to take advantage of our opportunities. How can we proceed on the grand march of industrial progress when our whole attention is absorbed with our inherent political complexities? Surely this settlement must be made and this question forever closed, so there will be nothing to distract our attention from the great question of developing the South in the manner which it deserves. That problem behind us, how easy will it be for us to grasp our imperial opportunities! The tyranny of the solid vote to be maintained on the one question is the most burdensome and exhausting which ever afflicted a people. Let us now cast it off.

More than this will arise out of the commercial change of to-day. As surely as we live, this marvellous industrial transformation of the South will sooner or later produce a division among us on the great questions of commerce. It is sure to do so. In every progressive Southern State, it has already made a division of the white voters. In my State, it has made an absolute and almost equal division of the vote. Under this condition of affairs, the Negro vote will count, and will surely be consulted. It is inevitable. We cannot put off the day. Then let that vote be intelligent and carry with it the dignity and consideration of property-owning and intelligence. Let the status of the voter be settled and the question will be out of the way and behind us. We do not wish to emulate the condition of affairs exemplified by the monarchies of Europe and be compelled to entirely devote our lives to the public safety.

Believing in the preservation of our civilization and holding to all the time-honored sentiments of the South, yet I believe that the changed condition of affairs to-day demands that the South should settle emphatically and once for all this great political question. Should prejudice stand in the way when almost rising to our splendid destiny? Should time-honored opinions interfere with our progress? Out from the shadows of the cloud, how glorious would be the light of our day! Relieved from its paralyzing effect, what country could equal our achievements! In the words of a great English statesman: "Or shall we expect from time, the physician of brutes, a lingering and uncertain deliverance? Shall we wait to be happy till we can forget that we are miserable, and owe to the weakness of our faculties a tranquillity which ought to be the effect of their strength? Far otherwise. Let us set all our past and present afflictions at once before our eyes. Let us resolve to overcome them, instead of flying from them, or wearing out the sense of them by long and ignominious patience. Instead of palliating remedies, let us use the incisive knife and the caustic, search the wound to the bottom, and work an immediate and radical cure."

A fair and honest franchise will once for all settle the question of Negro domination, the mere fear of which has been so great a blight to the South.

Delaying the settlement of the status of the Negro will, under the circumstances, but lose us precious time. The Negroes will in time become voters, full and free voters, and with our absolute and ultimate approbation and consent. Delay will not affect the final result. This may seem a bold statement, but if you will indulge me I will appeal to your experience for my justification.

Every argument of memory and experience teaches us that this question is surely solving itself in the ultimate direction of broad political liberty for the Negro. It is useless to controvert it. To-day, beyond denial, it is nearer a liberal solution than ever before. Under Providence, excepting the first great shock of civil franchise granted to the Negro, the other steps towards the broader enfranchisement have proceeded step by step, and under the assimilating and soothing process of time they have been without jar to our feelings or wound to the body politic. There has been no backward movement. It has been purely forward all the time. I challenge contradiction to this statement. I mean political and civil advancement. I adhere to absolute social and racial separation as earnestly as any one to whom I speak. Social and racial separation is the salvation of both races. Loose Memory's chain and wander with me over the South, enter the court-house and legislature and the marts of business, and you yourself will be amazed at your unconscious change of sentiment in the direction of liberality towards the

Negro. When he was a slave, we gave our fathers and sons to death, and deluged with blood this fair country to retain him as a slave; and yet within the sound of my voice there is not a man who, for all the land between the swelling seas, would rivet a fetter on the arm of a Negro. Stand with me in the sacred halls of Justice. I remember when a Negro's oath was not taken. Yet to-day an intelligent Negro on the witness-stand is accepted without question; and if he has been an honest man, no difference is made between him and a white man of equal character.

That which has distinguished the Anglo-Saxon in all times is the right of jury. The juryman must be a free man, and under the sun of Australia or the snows of the North, the jury has gone as the badge of the Anglo-Saxon. I remember when a Negro darkened no jury in my State; yet, to-day, Negro jurymen have been found by those experienced in the work of the court-house, to be, without question, safe and conservative.

In my town, with a prescience of the future beyond the wisdom of his day, Stonewall Jackson taught a Negro Sunday-school, at times against vehement protest and under threats of prosecution. To-day we have spent a hundred millions upon the Negro school, and not for the wealth of the Indies would we close them to him. In your business life his every step has been against a protest, but he has made his place within the march of affairs, and as great as the changes have been, they meet your and my approbation, showing the sure and almost unconscious progress to a widening sentiment for a most liberal solution of this political question in the direction I plead.

Then, sir, if the result of your experience points to the future as I have indicated, does not every reason of an intelligent and far-seeing statesmanship demand that we settle this status at once in the direction of an intelligent voting power? Does not the spirit of the day abroad in the land demand our wise and liberal action? Now arises an important question. If the South, far-seeing and liberal in its policy towards the Negro, should adopt a liberal franchise provision, can the Negro on his part ever become imbued with the American spirit? Will he ever become a citizen sufficiently intelligent so as to become a substantial integral portion of the American voting population? Will the progress shown on our part by the adoption of this free and equal basis of franchise meet any progress on the part of the Negro?

Are his feet on the ascending steps of a good citizenship? Is he improving in character, in religion, in material prosperity, in self-respect? Sir, I appeal to that tribunal which is more powerful for enlightenment than gathered statistics. I summon here as proofs the result of your own observation. I point to the spires rising heavenward all over this land and sheltering an increasing number of dusky and intelligent worshippers. I call here in witness the homes where, under their

own fig-tree and vine, live in plenty and sweet contentment increasing numbers of the Negro race. Yea,
Mr. Chairman, I point to the thousands of intelligent
students crowding the halls of learning in the South
and filling every situation open to them with credit
and character. I call to your attention a greater increase within the time in material prosperity than falls
to the lot of any other race excepting the Anglo-Saxon
in the wide world. I appeal to your own experience
as to the vast change for the better in the horde of
unlettered and ignorant Negroes within one generation. Within three generations mark his improvement
from the barbarian, bound and gyved, and thrust over
the side of the slave-ship and given to us. There has
been disappointment and discouragement, it is true,
but the progress has been substantial and on the right
line. I will not take your time with the discussion of
the detail of a proposition which is obvious to all.
I have given somewhat of study to the question of
his improvement, and a careful investigation of the
only people whose shackles within our time have been
broken, leads me to the conclusion, and it is the conclusion of every careful student of the emancipated
serfs of Russia, that the Negro has infinitely out-
progressed the freed white serf in every element of
an enlightened citizenship. Surely he has improved.
This has been the general consensus of opinion and
the observation and experience alike of the statesman,
the scholar, and the man of business of the South.

When I see the progress of the Negro and the sure improvement of the conditions surrounding him, the darkness which tinges the bright skies of the South brings me no despair. Out of the cloud should not come despair, but the sweet gladness of hope brightening our every difficulty. The evidences of His supreme care over us are too unmistakable for despair, and the cloud of witnesses that His care encompasses this nation, and that with the fingers of His wisdom he has placed these people among us, will admit of no question. When commerce languished and its utmost gates lay behind the white sails, and the rivers of India no longer gave their gold and the fields their gems, and the cunning hands of the East no longer wove the silk and garments of mankind, the treasury of plenitude of this new land yielded richer gems and gold more plentiful than ever glistened in Indian rivers or burdened with the glory of wealth the mines of Golconda. When the golden belt and the steel armor were the sole tokens of rule, when the king was the state and the people his servants, He gave to the world our country, where the only king is Freedom and where the People is the State. When under the rule of King and Cardinal and Noble the creed of the people was the voice of the Conclave, under the oaks of New England and the pines of Virginia there arose a thunderous song of a new people who cared not for the creed of Conclave, Diet, or Cardinal, and who heeded not the command of princes. When the swarthy

Spaniard, in leathern jerkin, found not the Fountain of Youth, for us its sweet waters waited lovingly and to-day are caressed for our good by the soft airs of our South. When Spain's covetous eyes, under casque and helmet, failed to find the gold of the West, and by its mighty power change human destiny, it was given to us to enrich our freedom with its plenitude beyond the wealth of kings. He gave us vast rivers on whose shores in the one season the fleecy cotton, the yellow corn, the golden wheat, the wine and the oil, the fruit and the flowers, the seed-time and the harvest, shed their glory. He flooded this land with the sunshine which on the prairie and beside the mountain kisses from the fertile field the grain and the fruit, and from His exhaustless plenty He has filled our land with the mighty agents of civilization waiting but our touch to garner them into the rich treasures of our commerce. He kept for this people the play of the lightning and imprisoned for us the giant arms of the steam. He has planned for us mighty continents and seas and lakes and rivers and harbors and capes, by whose power we can grasp in our strong hands the Ultima Thule of commerce. He strengthened the hands of tyrants that people from all countries forsaking their homes should give to us their best and their bravest ; and He broke to pieces the kings when they would shackle the progress and curb the holy aspirations of freedom and religion in this newest continent. In all the hoary ages He has filled the earth with tyrants and kings and has laid Africa close to their hands; yet, for reasons known only to His wisdom, He has reserved this free country as the land where the sigh of the slave and the rattle of his chain were more frequent than in any since the years began their race. For them He made peaceful fields incarnadined with the blood of a free people, yet over the carnage He made His Son to walk, and after His " Peace, be still," as on the troublous waters of Galilee, tenderness touched the heart and peace and unity and love passing all understanding reigned with the people. Then surely His mighty arms are around us and His Providence is with us. This thing, which we understand not and which our mortal eyes do not fully see, is for the ultimate glory of our people.

Whether this race surrounding us as a cloud, educated and strengthened to its full stature through our trials and our sorrows, shall, on the shores of the Tanganyika, raising the sweet songs of praise learned on the banks of the Tennessee, the Kanawha, and the Mississippi, lead the Dark Continent to the light of the brighter day, or whether as our helper here in fashioning this newest and best land, is not yet for mortal man to know. But, sir, with all my soul, I believe that this people has been placed here so as in some inscrutable manner to glorify this civilization so surely touched with the Master's fingers and so certainly fashioned with His hands. Ah, sir, there is no despair. The witnesses cannot fail.

3

Again, there is another reason why you should hurry the settlement of this franchise system and convert the Negro vote into an intelligent one as quickly as possible. With the exigencies of national life we, of the South, will ourselves shortly need the Negro vote. I look for the South to be as anxious to have the Negro vote counted as is the North to-day. The Negro vote heretofore has been allied to a political organization the bulk of whose existence is in the North and West. He has been generally opposed to the people among whom he lives. This has arisen for several reasons, that the Southern people were the people to whom he belonged as a slave, and for the further reason that he fell into the hands, during Reconstruction days, of those who preyed upon his credulity and ignorance and made him believe that the Southern people were his enemies. These impressions are rapidly losing their force and a newer and more intelligent class of Negroes is taking the place of the old. It is to me as plain as the open day that when the Negro is impressed with the idea that the white man of the South will treat him as fairly in politics as he does in business, he will gradually and surely incline to the support of the Southern people. It is inevitable. If this is not the case it is against the experience of all of the years. The Negro is drawing his living from the South. His every relation of life is with the Southern man. His existence is tied up with the Southern States. The laws generally enacted in the South are predicated upon the idea that the Negro will always vote against the Southern white man. This is a mistake. He will not. Nothing can be more certain than that he will ultimately become entirely affiliated with, and interested in, every policy of the Southern man. If the Negro does not become in time a good Southern man in every fibre of his being, he simply belies universal experience and breaks political precedent. When a question arises of sectional difference in the way of local policy in this country, as they are sure to arise in the Republic's life, you will need the Negro's vote and most surely you will get it. This condition is arising. It is rapidly coming. The South is no longer a great agricultural section, but it is becoming a great competitor with the North in all the commercial affairs of our national life. You will need every vote you can get to sustain your great commercial policies. The North will surely experience, as we have already experienced, the effect of the solid Negro vote. The South, most certainly, will be ultimately insistent that the Negro vote be counted. Then let the vote be an intelligent vote and let the question be settled and out of the way, and the Negro will be on the way to give us the assistance we shall certainly need.

This system will allow a different status of franchise in the different States of the Union according to the general condition of education and property-holding in each State. It will not act upon every State as an inflexible national constitutional provision. In one State, according to the rate of illiteracy and property-holding, it will exclude a larger element of the population than in another State.   In the other State, if there is a different ratio of illiteracy and property-holding, then a fair ratio of the population of that State would be touched by its provisions, thus acting fairly and equitably upon the peculiar conditions of each State.

There is another and higher aspect of this question to be considered.   By the ancestral clause in many States you pull the white man down, and with an educational franchise you push the Negro to the highest educational exercise.   You place a premium upon the ignorance of the white man of the South.   You say to him that there must be a higher educational basis for the Negro, and yet the white man can attain the highest rights of American citizenship and at the same time wallow in ignorance.   It is a wrong to the white man, which will surely bear its fruit.   I have not understood in my investigation of the Anglo-Saxon that he needs to have any handicap put on any other race.

Mr. Chairman, the franchise system, as it is at present constituted in many of the States in the South, is, to say the least, practically the policy of repression. Repression has been tried at every age of the world's history and always with the same unvarying result —utter and tremendous failure.   It leads nowhere.   It raises no man.   It demands no education.   It holds ignorance as dense as ever.   It drives away intelligence.   It breeds discontent.   It represses any rising aspiration of the heart. It leaves the land at the end of the cycle just as it found it at the beginning. It is the policy of deadly inaction overridden by discontent. It has filled the rich empire of Russia with the nihilist and the anarchist, where your brother is a spy upon your life and the highest official of the court touches arms with the serf to plot destruction to the government. It has gangrened and filled beautiful Ireland with seething discontent. In every country the system has borne the same terrible results. In our country, where every man, white and black, feels that he has the right to equal law, under such a system the effect is increased a thousand-fold. Only the other day I stood in the little room where the mighty spirit of Stonewall Jackson wrestled in its last conflict with the Great Ruler. The scene which occurred there in the old troublous days arose to my mind. With his life-blood ebbing, his thoughts were still on the battle-field in the conflict for his beloved country. As his immortal spirit left his body, those around him were thrilled by his last commands here on earth : "General, you must keep your men together and hold your ground!" My fellow-countrymen, under this system, can you hold the glory and the civilization of the South together? I ask you who believe in exact justice, in representative government, can you under the present system hold your ground? Would the kindly eyes under the old worn hat countenance the continuance of the system of political government where, even if it was once necessary, that necessity in the change of affairs in this Republic has long since departed? The answer coming from every true patriot and far-seeing man of the South is, there is but one way for the South to keep our men together and hold our ground, and that is behind a fair, honest, and equitable system bearing alike upon every one.

Is not this course demanded by the plainest dictates of prudence? Does it not appeal to the most elemental principles of foresight? We have the alternative plainly presented to us. Place the franchise on a fair and wise and permanent basis or leave it in its present condition of unrest. Which is best for the South? Which plan does true patriotism prescribe? Which appeals to statesmanship and which appeals to the hour? The train of evils waiting on the present condition is too apparent for controversy. The open demand in high places for the absolute disfranchisement of the Negro, leaving ten millions of people without hope in the midst of our nation; the argument presented for the repeal of the Fifteenth Amendment, which would again rend in twain this great nation; the natural discontent resulting from the growing intelligence of the Negro; the reiterated resolutions presented to Congress unfairly representing us to the world of commerce and justice; the demand for the reduction of our representation, are all practical results of the unsettled condition of our franchise. What do we gain by delay? Nothing. We will only miss our opportunity to grasp the decisive moment for action, and with the opening of the new era of industrial change to reorganize our franchise system. When it begins and is under way, it is too late.

> "New times, new climes, new lands, new men, but still
> The same old tears, old wrongs, and oldest ill."

Shall we longer wait? Is not the fair settlement of this question in the manner I have indicated far wiser than any attempt to repeal or modify the Fifteenth Amendment, which has been so ably pressed by a respected member of this Conference? Will you allow me an additional moment to oppose, with all the earnestness of my life, this last proposition? At the risk of overtaxing your indulgence, I beg your further attention. This proposition is too powerfully and seductively urged by my friend, Dr. Murphy, to be passed in silence. We are striving to close the gulf between the two great sections. This demand would again open wide the bitterness of the olden days. It would say to the North, as Abraham of old said to Lot: "Separate thyself, I pray thee, from me. If thou wilt take the left hand, then I will go to the right; but if thou wilt depart to the right hand, then I will go to the left." It would be a step backward. It would be practically a revolution. It would loose from its moorings the crystallized sentiment of a third of a century. It would practically again raise the issues of the war. It could result only in evil by agitation, for it could never be accomplished. It would require the affirmative vote of the majority of the Legislatures of three-fourths of the States to repeal the amendment. It would require two-thirds of the vote of the Senate of the United States and the House of Representatives. The majority of one branch of the Legislature of only twelve States can defeat its modification or repeal. One-third vote in the House or Senate would defeat the repeal. No human right in all the history of government is so absolutely guaranteed as the rights under the Amendments to the Constitution. The practical effect of the repeal would be to wrest from the South a portion of our representation, which we could not consider in this day of industrial progress and need.

Sir, there is a higher reason than the loss of representation. The repeal or modification of the Fifteenth Amendment means the practical turning over to the South of the Negro Question as a local question. Are we able to bear it? Is not the question of the political status of ten millions of a different race, living amidst us, burden sufficient for the whole nation, which can only be settled, under the providence of the Almighty, by the earnest, hearty, and loving co-operation of the North and South? This action would, as nothing else, destroy that kindly co-operation.

With all our strength and pride, is not the burden too great for us alone to bear? We have trodden the winepress so long and our feet are worn with the weary round of the threshing-floor. I know that it is fashionable to say: " Hands off! the South will settle its race troubles in its own way!" It seems to me that those who echo this cry know not what they say and do not understand the burden which they would impose upon our strength, and surely the love of our reunited country has not yet flooded their hearts with its tender beauty and power. It is true that the fructification of our hopes seems almost a dream touched with the radiance of the glory of that Blessed Land where alone the sunshine is brighter and the day more translucent than that which illumines and glorifies our own South. It is true that with a robe radiant and gorgeous with the waving grain, the fragrant hemp, the snowy cotton, and the ripened grape, we have clothed the nakedness of the dear old land. We have filled the desolate places with laughter and happiness and plenty, and with the sweet alchemy of the passing years as our gentle handmaiden, have poured the healing nepenthe upon the broken heart. Amid the fatness of our fields and beside our rivers, whose waters, like the minor strains of sad music, incessantly voice hallowed associations, and whose shores are redolent with the memories of sorrows endured and trials overcome, we are again erecting a majestic civilization. Yet, notwithstanding this glory of our labor, do we not need all of the tender sympathy and loving interest and wise counsel which our brother of the North holds out to us with an open hand and a generous heart? This is the question in the economy of our governmental life which cannot be local. Its settlement concerns all of the country, North and South alike. The South more immediately and acutely, it is true, but equally in its far-reaching consequences it touches all the people. It should not be left to the South to work it out alone and unaided. I am as insistent as any son of the South can be upon our supreme right to settle in our own way our social affairs, and I insist that in our social and racial treatment of the question our hands should be free to fend as meets our need. That aspect is local and personal. However, upon the great question of its final settlement in its national aspect, it will take all of the united wisdom and resources of the whole people. Why should not this supreme question have the undivided labor of our reunited and loving people, rendered almost omnipotent in the grandeur of its accomplishment, because the endeavor is crowned and glorified by the Brotherhood which, with each fading sunset, grows sweeter and dearer as the sullen crimson lights of the sad past

"Tinge the sober twilight of the Present
With color of romance"?

Well remembering what in our nakedness and emptiness we have accomplished in the settlement of the Race Question, yet I make obeisance to those of the North who by their assistance have rendered it possible for the South to have accomplished so much. With all my soul I plead that with us no narrow spirit of sufficiency or suspicion of untoward interference on the part of the North should prevent the intertwining of our lives and our energies in the unravelling of the complexities of a situation which more vitally affects modern civilization than any question of the present day. For us to do so was for Theseus to refuse the sword of Ariadne, and to cast aside the skein of silk proffered by the loving hand of the daughter of Minos. A follower of Him, the latchet of whose shoe we are not worthy to loose, relates that on one of the carnage-stricken fields of old Virginia an officer of a Massachusetts regiment lay wounded to death. His regiment had passed on leaving him alone with the fading light and amid the quickly-coming shadows. He was lying in the line of the march of the Southern troops, and as a Southern soldier hurried by he called and asked him to pray with him. "Oh, I am sorry I cannot," he said ; " I have never learned to pray for myself." Yet with soft hands and tender sympathy he placed the dying officer under the grateful shade, pillowed his head, and cooling his fevered lips with water from his canteen, he left him with words of cheer and hurried away to the battle-field. Soon the ears almost in hearing of the majestic music of that better land and rendered doubly acute by its near approach, again heard coming footsteps, and as another Southern soldier passed by the pleading lips called out, "I beg you to come and pray with me." Seeing the dimming eyes and the broken form, the Southern soldier

knelt down beside his erstwhile foeman and poured
over that battle-stricken field his prayer for the guidance of one about entering the encircling shadows, and
for the sweet and divine consolation of those dear ones
he had left at home.   As the man of the South prayed,
there came to the wistful, fast-closing eyes a vision of
the homestead in the North, with the old mother looking down the flower-bordered lane and listening for
footsteps too long in their returning ; the well, with
its sweet water, under the shadow of the waving elms ;
the sweet meadow, with its fragrance of newly-cut
grass and flowers ; the children at their little play ;
the evening table and the vacant chair, and the sweet-
faced waiting wife with the little one in her arms ;
and with each supplication and sweet reminder of life
and loved ones and of the nearer and other life, the
weakening arms, clothed in their uniform of blue,
wrapped themselves around the gray-clad soldier.
Nearer and nearer crept the wounded form in blue,
and as the last tender supplication went out to the
Throne from the lips of the Southerner, the spirit of
the soldier of the North went on its journey and left
its mortality, holding in close embrace the gray-clad
soldier of the South.

And here, my countrymen, in this splendid presence, I invoke, as a touchstone to our lives and a
guide to our feet, often wandering, that spirit of unity
of love and action which touched the battle-fields with
the tenderness of unseen hands and gave amidst the

lonely pines of old Virginia a foretaste of the spirit of better days yet to come.

Then, sir, let us approach this supremest question of our civil life with hearts touching and arms about each other and strengthened by a consecrated union of purpose and interest, and we will, as conquerors, ascend those imperial heights of self-abnegation, patriotism, and true statesmanship, where amidst the blooming of sweet flowers of love and perfect trust we will contemplate a happy people undivided by internecine conflict and unshaken by sectional difference. Yea, we will not approach this question with broken bodies clothed with the blue and the gray, and over fields strewn with the ruck of a despairing civilization, tinged with the dun colors of sectional conflict and difference; but rather as brothers whose endeavor is illumined by the golden sunlight encompassing the rich cities, the fields abounding with fertility, the advancing commerce and civil glory of a united people. Conscious of the ultimate rectitude of an enlightened nation and touched with the spirit of Him who taught as never man taught the unchangeable principles of right and justice to all men of every condition, we together, the North and the South, will work out to its finality this great problem, in love, in justice, and in moderation, to the glory of our civilization, and leave to our children's children the priceless illustration of a people forgetting the sorrows and hatreds of other days, surrendering sectional advantage, doing equal justice to every man of every color and condition, and resolutely turning the face to a day of wider and better and brighter and more glorious national life which will hasten the time when justice will be the delight of our people and the chiefest glory of our free government!

II

THE RACE QUESTION

THE question which we have for consideration to-day is the Negro Question in its relation to the practical affairs of the South. Discussing the Negro from a practical standpoint, you must discuss the settlement of the Race Question. With the Race Question on its way to settlement, the practical evolution will quickly come. As soon as it is understood that this question is of the past, then will immediately begin the industrial evolution of the South. What we want is a practical and final method of settlement of the question as between the two races. When that is determined, there is no question as to the South, with its wonderful natural advantages, taking care of the whole practical question. That being my view, I propose to discuss the best plan of finally determining the Race Question. With the South unhampered by this great question, there will be no trouble about the mills and the manufactories and the industrial affairs of the South.

To the practical men who desire the upbuilding of the South, the time has come to speak plainly and honestly. The Race Question, however, is no longer a question of the South. It is a question of the whole country, and it is affecting the whole body politic. As a matter of material interest, the greatest outlay of money within ten years in this country has been made in the South. This is largely Northern money. The greatest development of the nation's prosperity, naturally speaking, within ten years has been in the South. The South is no longer industrially a back-door, no longer a *terra incognita*. With one exception, the finest developments of iron ore are in the South, and the largest body of hardwood timber is in the South. One State in the South has more coal than Pennsylvania and Ohio combined. One State in the South is to-day exceeding Pennsylvania in the production of oil; one Southern State is the second coke producer, and it ranks third in the production of coal. There is more water-power in one State in the South than there is in the whole of New England. In her ability to manufacture cheap textiles, she has no competitor. In every branch of natural mercantile supremacy she is easily the first.

The race of trade and of civilization is to-day inexorable, and the cheapest and best will win in the industrial warfare. The West is teeming with population. It is largely agricultural in its nature. The South, unlike the West, affords a varied field for agricultural, mineral, and manufacturing development. The North, with the quick intuition of trade, understands this, and to-day it is concerned in the South, not alone from a question of patriotism for the whole country, but also from the fact that millions of Northern money have been poured into the South, and the sons and daughters of the North are with us as part and parcel of our political, economic, and social existence. Therefore, I say that the North from a mere practical standpoint is interested as well as the South in all of the complexities of the Race Question.

As to actual development in the South I will be pardoned for a moment. Within ten years, the greatest number of railroads have been developed in the South. Within ten years, more mills and factories have been erected in the South than in any other part of the country. Within ten years, more cities have been founded and more towns have grown into great cities than in any other part of the United States. Within ten years, there has been a greater change of immigration towards the South than towards any other part of the United States. So I reiterate, that it is a national question that we are confronting. What are we to do about it? With the great practical genius of the American people, there is no question about our ability to grapple with it. Let us not refine. Let us discuss the question plainly, yet with mutual and decent forbearance both for the white and for the black and for the North and for the South.

In the first place, we must disabuse the mind in each section of the prejudice which surrounds the Race Question. I speak as a Southern man who springs from two hundred years of Southern ancestry, and am naturally filled with the prejudice of the South. The Southern men generally believe that the enfranchisement of slaves at the Reconstruction period was entirely from hate, viciousness, and revenge on the part of the Northern people. A great many of the Northern people have the idea that the whole object of the Southern man is to nullify the *post-bellum* amendments to the Constitution and practically to re-enslave the black ; that there was no great or salient question of race instinct or race supremacy, and that the Southern man's treatment of the Negro after the war was intended as an insult to the North ; that the Ku-Klux plan was purely for revenge and wanton spirit and not for protection. Now, as a matter of fact, neither one of these propositions is correct. A majority of the Northern people in their idea of reconstruction were honest, and their desire for the complete emancipation of the slaves was the influence behind them. To some extent there was a vast deal of narrowness and ignorance among the Northern people, but as a Southern man I do not believe that the horrors of reconstruction were for the mere purpose of revenge or viciousness on the part of the Northern people. A great number of the political leaders, misinforming and misleading the Northern people, were largely responsible for these wrongs ; but I do not believe that the mass of the people in the North intended to wantonly injure and degrade the South.

On the other hand, the Southern man was confronted

with the most gigantic problem that had ever fallen to a people. With an ignorant, superstitious, and alien race in absolute control of his home, holding control of his State government, directing the affairs of his city, wrecking and looting the State, devastating the fields, destroying the schools, and asserting itself ignorantly in all of the affairs of the State, he was naturally restive, and did things which to the Northern eye and to the Northern mind were not demanded by the circumstance of the situation. To the credit of both North and South, however, the situation is daily being better understood. In the North they are beginning to understand that there is a great question which concerns both sections, the South, more nearly, because the South is the seat of the trouble. The South, on its side, has gotten its bearings, laid out its ground, and is more thoroughly understanding the situation and how to deal with it. Therefore, there is before us an actual question of vast moment, and it is our duty as honest men to give it the best consideration of our lives, so that it may be settled for the glory of this great civilization. Many methods have been suggested of settling the question. Much has been written and said upon the subject. We will take each proposed remedy and discuss it separately. What are they?

1. Colonization, domestic and foreign.
2. Diffusion.
3. Absorption or Amalgamation.

To some extent I ask to be pardoned for a discussion

of these general plans.   I do so for the reason that as quickly as possible the whole of the country should be united upon one conservative plan for the settlement of the Race Question.   I do not propose to go into detail. It will no doubt be disappointing that I discuss this question in the manner I propose, but in my judgment every plan should be thoroughly discussed in order that the best one may obtain.   Dissipation of ideas is the destruction of our purpose, and it has heretofore largely impeded progress in the practical affairs of the South. Numbers of honest, zealous, and sincere men working upon different plans have accomplished very little, and it is our duty, if at all possible, to combine our theories into a practical unity of plan.   When we settle upon a plan as an absolute finality, and all work along those lines, wonders will result.   To accomplish this by honest and plain statements seems to be the best.   Let us see what are the weak points of the general plan of this settlement of the question.   When the acute stage is passed, the practical will immediately appear.   When the mind has become settled, the whole body politic can go to work, and thus material advancement will be the immediate result.   I base my whole argument upon the idea that in the South the Negro will live.   He is here to stay.   We had just as well make up our minds to that effect.   A number of intelligent peo-ple, backed by powerful sentimental influence, look to colonization as the best settlement.   It is the oldest idea, and one upon which vasts sums of money have been spent. Is it practicable? Let us consider it.

First we will take the question of domestic colonization, which means, in the language of one of its greatest disciples, "the purchasing or procuring of a territory within our limits, erecting it into a statehood and placing thereon all of the colored population of the United States." This is a dream of the brightest colors, yet but a dream. This plan of late has many and eminent followers in this country. The carrying out of the statehood plan involves the settlement of greater questions than confront us in the Race Question.

First consider the question of property. The Negro of the South owns three hundred and fifty thousand farms and homes without incumbrance. He is paying taxes on four hundred million dollars' worth of property. He has great possessions in churches, schools, and colleges. In a thousand ways he is intermingled in the vast rights of innumerable business affairs.

With either foreign or domestic colonization, how are you going to get rid of the Negro's property. Sell it? Confiscate it? Force him to sell it? Nay, verily. To do so you have to change the Constitution of the United States and also of the States in which the Negro largely lives. He is under the protection of the Constitutions, National and State. Under the Constitution of the United States, you cannot interfere with his status except for crime. The men generally who propose the exportation of the Negro for the reason that his civil and political status is not recognized in the South, are in favor of taking him without his consent, absolutely destroying his civil status, and removing him from his home and placing him in another habitation. Speaking practically, how are the statehood dreamers going to get rid of the law of the land, which protects every citizen of this Republic in his home, his liberty, and his country? Plainly speaking, to carry out the plan means the forcible abduction of the Negro race. To leave it to their consent means that the vast majority will not consent to go, and thus the question is not solved. The question teems with difficulties beside which the Race Question is but small. Again, the view of one of the greatest exponents of this idea is to take part of what is known as the arid regions of this country and place thereon the Negro. To be perfectly frank, I think that after the two centuries of vassalage of the Negro, after the wrongs which have been committed upon him, to take him away from his vine and fig-tree, and place him in the arid region of the country would be as great a crime as our enslaving him. Another proposition. There are in this country practically nine millions of Negroes. This is a vast number. How could we erect that number into a statehood? Let us consider a moment. The most populous State we have is New York State. It has a little upwards of six millions of people. The next in population is Pennsylvania with upwards of five millions of people. The State of New York has an area of

49,000 square miles. The State of Pennsylvania has 45,000 square miles. Here are two congested States in whose borders the whole civilization of this country has had full play for two centuries, yet there are in these two great States but few more than one-half the number of people than there are negroes in the whole country. I will ask some one who believes in the separate statehood of the Negroes to show us where this extent of territory could be procured. The Northwestern States, in Oregon, Utah, Nebraska, Dakota? From an economic standpoint it is well known that the Negro could not live in this, to him, inhospitable region. He is a creature of the South, and alone in the South can he live. Then, again, how will you procure the territory of the State in which he is to live? By reconstruction? By the destruction of one State and the reconstruction of another? By dismembering sovereignty? Consider for a moment the constitutional limitations of our country. Will any State consent to be dismembered in order that a population necessarily ignorant and inferior shall be placed within its limits? The only method by which you could dismember a State would be with the consent of the people within the State. What State in the Union would consider for a moment its dismemberment in order that it might be created into separate statehood for the Negro? The question is greater than the Race Question. Again, the scheme of domestic colonization means that the

Negroes shall alone inhabit the State. How will you rid the State to be taken of the citizens who have carved its statehood out of the wilderness and who have planted their own civilization within its borders? By the right of eminent domain, forsooth! If that is done, we must change the Constitution. Are we willing to submit ourselves to the throes of other amendments to the Constitution for the settlement of this question? It would produce a greater rocking of the State than the Reconstruction Acts. Then the idea seems to be to place the Negro by himself in his own territory and under his own control. The best men in the North and in the South who have considered this subject believe that it is not right that the American nation should turn the Negro race over to itself at this period of its evolution. In my judgment, the Negro is not ready to be left to himself. It is the duty of the people who brought him here to stand by him and help him in the evolution of this great race problem. Gentlemen, how long, with the fecundity of the Negro race, would his increase be confined within the borders of his State? How long before the government would be called upon to purchase other States for him in the natural order of increase?

Another suggestion : How would it be possible to keep the white man out and the Negro in? The borders of the Negro State would have to be surrounded by the musket and the bayonet. Then take the political question. Those who are in favor of this segregation of the Negro seem to be largely in favor of the proposition by reason of his loss of political rights in the South. Pray tell me what political rights and power would he have, representing one State in the whole sisterhood of States? That State would practically be an alien State. What power would he have for improvement? What ability would he have to obtain from the National Government the recognition which his numbers would ordinarily demand? When he is situated among the white race, that which the white race receives from the Government is divided with him. Situated as he would be in his own State and by himself, it would be practically nine millions of black people confronted by seventy millions of white people, and he would receive nothing of the recognition which he receives to-day. Then the expense, if you would consider the question of expense of the exodus of nine millions of people. In all the history of the moving of nations, such an exodus as this has never been accomplished.

Let us discuss foreign colonization.

1st. As I have before said, how will you get the consent of the American Negro to his deportation to a foreign land? He is a citizen, and without his consent you cannot take away his rights. Consider a moment the question of expense. It would at the lowest estimate cost in mere transportation more than five hundred millions of dollars, with at least a similar amount to prepare him to go and to sustain him for a time when there. It would take at least thirty years to a half a century in time. To settle the machinery of the movement would take longer than the settlement of the Race Question by rational methods within our own country. Again, the great religious and philanthropic sense of the great American nation would revolt against the deportation of nine millions of Negroes to Central America or to Africa. Practically, with few exceptions, it would mean, in their present state of social and economic development, the turning back to the barbarism of Africa, which is too revolting for discussion, and the Southern people, upon whom to-day falls the greatest burden of the race, who are to-day the greatest sufferers from the racial question, would not permit it. The North would not consent. It would be such a crime that the crime of slavery would pale into insignificance thereby. Many men suggest acquiring by treaty or purchase territory in South or Central America and thereon locating the Negro. In the first place, I do not believe that any government, even among the wretched, mixed, dictator-ridden states of Central America would permit us to unload on them our burden. There will also come the great question of protecting the purchased state, and there will arise all of the complications of our relation to its government, and with it all the endless questions springing from the government of the mongrel state among the nations of South America.

I have heard it stated by respectable authorities that

many Negroes are clamoring to be exported to Africa. I live among the Negroes, and to my oft-repeated question as to whether they would be willing to go, I have not as yet gotten from one intelligent Negro an affirmative answer.

It would seem to me that the non-partisan statement of the Educational Bureau of the United States would be sufficient evidence to do away with the question of massing the Negroes either in foreign colonization or in domestic statehood. Says the able Commissioner "In educational and in industrial progress this race has accomplished more than it could have achieved if settled in different environments without the aid of the whites. The Negro has needed the experience as well as the aid of the white man. In sections where the colored race has been massed and removed from contact with the whites, the progress of the Negro has been retarded. He is an imitative being, and has a constant desire to attempt whatever he sees the white man do. He believes in the education of his children, because he can see that an increase of knowledge will enable them to better their condition. The Bureau shows that in States where the colored population is highest in proportion to the total population, or where such population is massed in the 'Black Belt,' as in South Carolina, Alabama, Mississippi, and Louisiana, there the per cent. of illiteracy is highest."

I would suggest that this reason alone would be

potent in settling the Race Question by sending the Negro to himself to live in his own ignorance.

In addition to the crime of removal, I repeat that the Negro sent back into Africa in his present state of evolution would simply mean a relapse in his status of civilization. I do not mention this as a case of race inferiority. I do not mean to include in this statement all of the race. There are Negroes who have reached a high degree of intellectuality, but I say in all frankness to send the Negro back to Africa in his present condition would be the crime of the world. The experiment has been tried and it is a horrible failure. In the West Indies and in Liberia we have had examples of what many friends of the Negro race—among others, my distinguished and able friend, the Senator from North Carolina—are insisting should be done with the American Negro. With no intention of depreciating the Negro's ability for self-government, but two examples are sufficient. Take Liberia, upon which state there has been poured millions of dollars by the friends of the Negro; where the highest statesmanship has provided him with a government and a habitation. Here we find a dreadful failure. Says the late minister to Liberia, an intelligent man :

"They have no money or currency in circulation of any kind. They have no boats of any character, not even a canoe. The two gunboats England gave them lie rotten on the beach. They have no guns or swords in working condition, nor even a cannon to fire a salute, though they purchased at one time 47,000 dollars' worth of guns from the United States.

. . . .

"There are only four post-offices in the country, one for each of the four counties. The government has no harbor, wharf, or breakwaters for steamers to land at. The next morning I looked for manufactories, mills, shops, artisan establishments of some kind, furnishing employment to the masses. Not one of any description could be found. I enquired for a hotel. They told me that there was none. No tailor-shop, no blacksmith to make a nail, no tinner to make a cup, no jeweller to set your watch; nothing to amuse you, nothing to engage your time, nothing to keep you in earnest. Look from morning till night, and you will never see a horse, a mule, a donkey, or oxen. They have none. There is not a buggy, a wagon, a cart of any kind, or a wheelbarrow in the four counties. The natives carry everything on their heads. . . . There are one hundred nude persons to every one wearing clothes. They have no statute against indecent exposure. . . . The government contains no public schools of any kind. The missionary schools teach the natives' children exclusively, when the people in this country and in England have expended in Liberia for education and improvement near $7,000,000. If everything in Liberia was sold excepting the individuals, not more than $1,000,000 could be realized. The Colonization Society claims to have aided 22,000 civilized Negroes to go to

Liberia since they first went there in 1822. To-day, in
the whole of Liberia, in a population, native and civilized, of fully 1,000,000, only 12,000 can be said to be
civilized."

Take our own continent, and a glance at the island
of San Domingo shows a similar condition of affairs
in that beautiful island, when left to the absolute
control of the Negro race in its present system of evolution. I quote from Mr. Froude's book, *The English in
the West Indies.*

"St. Domingo, of which Hayti is the largest division,
was the earliest island discovered by Columbus, and the
finest in the Carribean Ocean. The Spaniards found
there a million or two of mild and innocent Indians,
whom they converted off the face of the earth—working
them to death in their mines and plantations. They
filled their places with blacks from Africa. They
colonized ; they built cities ; they throve and prospered
for nearly two hundred years, when Hayti was taken
from them and made a French province. The French
kept it till the revolution. They built towns ; they
laid out farms and sugar fields ; they planted coffee all
over the island, where it now grows wild. Vast herds
of cattle roamed over the mountains ; splendid houses
rose over the rich savannahs. The French church
put out its strength ; there were churches and preachers
in every parish. So firm was the hold that they had
gained, that Hayti, like Cuba, seemed to have been
made a part of the old world, and as civilized as France

herself. The revolution came, and the reign of liberty. The blacks took arms ; they surprised the plantations ; they made a clean sweep of the whole French population. The island being thus derelict, Spain and England both tried their hand to recover it, but failed, and a black nation, with a republican constitution, and a population perhaps of about one million and a half of pure blood Negroes, has since been in unchallenged possession, and has arrived at the condition which has been described to us by Sir Spencer St. John.

" Morals in the technical sense they have none ; but they cannot be said to sin, because they have no knowledge of a law. They are naked and not ashamed. They sin ; but they sin only as animals, without shame, because there is no sense of doing wrong. In fact, those poor children of darkness have escaped the consequences of the fall, and must have come of another stock after all. Immorality is so universal that it almost ceases to be a fault . . . it is the rule. In spite of schools and missionaries, seventy per cent. of the children now born among them are illegitimate. Young people make experiment of one another before they will enter into any closer connection. So far they are no worse than our own English islands, where the custom is equally general ; but behind the religiosity, there lies as active and alive the horrible revival of the West African superstitions ; the serpent worship, and the child sacrifice, and the cannibalism. The facts are notorious. . . . A few years ago, persons guilty of these infamies were tried and punished; now they are left alone, because to prosecute and convict them would be to acknowledge the truth of the indictment.

" The blacks as long as they were slaves were docile and partly civilized . . . but the effect of leaving the Negro nature to itself is apparent at last. There is no sign, not the slightest, that the generality of the race are improving either in intelligence or moral habits; all of the evidence is the other way. The generality are mere good-natured animals. The customs of Dahomey have not yet shown themselves in the English West Indies, and never can while the English authority is maintained; but no custom of any kind will be found in a Negro hut or village from which his most sanguine friend can derive a hope that he is on the way to mending himself. Ninety years of Negro self-government have had their use in showing what it really means. The movement is backward, not forward."

I am sorry to make these quotations, but I am making in this address a plain statement of facts and am not dealing with sentiment. We are discussing the facts without regard to sentiment, and I believe that when the facts are well understood the intelligence and philanthrophy of the American people will not support a very large and intelligent class of people who believe that colonization is the settlement of this question. Mark you, I do not make this quotation for the purpose of showing that the Negro race cannot rise to a high degree of civilization. I believe that with the right guidance it will be one of the factors in the world's affairs.

Now arises the kindred question. If you do not colonize these people how will you save the country from their natural increase? Will they not overwhelm and become the dominant race, thus displacing the Anglo-Saxon civilization? This argument is often heard and often believed. Many people are of the opinion that the Negro from mere natural increase will become the dominant race factor in the South. The statistics do not bear out this fear of a great relative increase of the Negro. I do not believe that this danger threatens us. Further than this every indication points to the fact that the Gulf of Mexico will be an American sea, that we will practically have control of the islands of the Gulf of Mexico. This seems to me our ultimate destiny. Every condition of business foresight, commercial and military strategy, seems to point in that direction. Since the events of the last year I am more impressed by the suggestion that in addition to Cuba and Porto Rico we should have under our control Hayti and San Domingo. Many of the educated blacks of this country will then naturally turn to these islands where their labor in every sphere is at a premium, and where they can live better and easier and be more efficient than in any other part of the world, excepting Africa. Numbers of them in time will naturally go to the southern islands, where by reason of their natural condition they will be of vast use in the work of regenerating the rich islands of the southern seas. I further believe that the nations under the providence of God are working out in Africa the destiny of the African race. At the present state of his intelligence the Negro cannot, unaided and alone, contend with the difficulties of African settlement and colonization. He cannot plan by himself, but Africa is being developed under the immediate control of the white race, who are building railroads into those regions and who are supervising its evolution from barbarism and savagery to civilization. This is being done by nations powerful from a military and commercial standpoint, and who are able to afford the protection and pay the money to do the vast work. Here will be one of the great fields and one of the homes of the civilized African race. Not being forced or deported thousands of them will go back and assist the nations of the earth in the development of their people.

The great nations which are at the present developing Africa will have need for exactly the people whom we are educating upon the American soil at this time, and I believe that many will find congenial work in developing the great African Continent. This does not militate against my view of *en masse* colonization. One is forced, the other is natural and symmetrical and comes when the people who are able to do the work are fit for the labor which is set before them. They will not be turned loose in the wilds of Africa, but will go there under the superior organizing ability of the white man to work out the destiny of the Negro race. I believe numbers of them will go to the African Continent, but here in the South will be the home of the great body of the race and the questions must be worked out with that cardinal principle always in view.

Another sure and certain relief from the over-burden of a large colored population will come by reason of the unprecedented commercial and manufacturing growth of the South. This will to a great extent restore the numerical relation between the two races in the South. If the same condition of commercial activity continues in the South within the next ten years as has been witnessed in the last ten years, vast numbers of manufactories of all kinds, in all of the various industries of iron and wood, marble, steel, and of the textiles, will herein have their place. This will cause cities to grow, manufactories to rise, and will bring about all of the active commercial environments of the Northern manufacturer. This will surely carry with it the influx of a large and active white population which will act as a balance to the present congestion of the Negro race. The present limits of the " Black Belt " would easily allow to live within it a population as large as the population of the United States, and the race conditions would be entirely reversed. Under the theories which I have advanced as to the predominance of the white and at the present time more intelligent person, the Race Question would be put in the background. In addition to this, the presence of an active, energetic, manufacturing, white citizenship would bring about a great solving of the question, in that it would have a vast effect upon the intelligence of the weaker race. We do not fear the intelligent black man.   It is the ignorant member of his race who is troublesome.

I will say just here that it has been shown by the most careful researches that there is not the great danger in the increase of the Negroes as has heretofore been supposed. The Senator from Massachusetts, when he speaks of fifty millions of Negroes in the Southern country within a generation, is entirely out of plumb with the facts.   The Negro in proportion to the white man shows a diminished increase in numbers. It appears from the most accurate census tables that a century ago the population of the South was made up of whites and Negroes in the proportion of 65 and 35 per cent., and that, in 1890, the proportion was 69 and 31 per cent.   The proportion of Negroes increased to 1810, when it reached 37 per cent., leaving only 63 per cent. as the proportion of whites, and this remained stationary for thirty years.   Since 1810 the proportion of Negroes has diminished.   That is, for the first half of the century the Negro population increased more rapidly than the whites, while during the last half of the century they have increased proportionately less rapidly than the whites, and, in proportion to the numbers, they are diminishing.   The whites have increased in a century to the census year of 1890 from three millions to fifty-five millions, and the Negroes from three-fourths of a million to seven millions five hundred thousand. The whites in 1890 were eighteen times as numerous as in 1790; the Negroes only ten times as numerous. In 1790 they were 19.27 of the whole population, and in 1890 they were only 11.93 of the total population. Excepting the defective census of 1880 and the census of 1810, every census report shows that the Negro is falling behind the white man in the rate of increase, thus showing beyond any doubt that the white race is more and more becoming the numerically dominant race. The most careful investigations settle the fact that the dominant civilization will be the white civilization, and the plain figures dispel the spectre of the numerical black control in this country and in the South.

A kindred method to colonization is the question of Diffusion, which has all the objections with even less of the advantages of the other plans. This plan, mark you, is proposed by those who believe that the rights of the Negro, political and otherwise, are not respected by his white brethren in the South. The idea is practically to take away from him by diffusion in other communities in other States any power for danger which he may have, thus rendering him a small factor in a large community. In other words the idea is to destroy him entirely as a political, economic, or social factor. The practical method, as I understand it, from those with whom I have discussed this subject, is to say to a certain number of Negroes, we will place you in different portions of the United States. 500,000 of you will go

to Ohio; 100,000 to Dakota; 100,000 will go to Cali-
fornia, and so on.   Here arise all of the great questions
I have before discussed without any of the advantages.
How will you procure the land in the different parts of
the country upon which to place the discitizenized and
deported Negroes?   How will you get the consent of
the people now living upon the lands to move out and
give their homes to the Negro race?   I will be pardoned
for not discussing this subject further.

Then, again, there is another method, and that is the
Absorption of the Negro race by the whites.   Throw
down all of the laws against inter-marriage of the white
and black.   Destroy all of the social laws affecting the
equality or inequality of the races.   Open the doors of
the churches, of the family, and of the home, to white
and black promiscuously.   Do away with the white
race by an absolute interchange of blood with the black,
and let all be reduced to one level or raised to one
height in the commingling of the two races.   Let us
consider this idea.   What has been the effect of commingling of the two races one upon the other?   I will
not discuss this branch of the subject with any idea that
there is any hope of its being adopted.   I discuss it for
the reason that it is one of the remedies prominently
suggested.   The South would never consider it.   That
is absolute, and I give it a place in my discussion to-day
so that I can in some degree contribute my mite in
showing that it is not feasible and should not be considered.   It is too horrible for contemplation.   This is

practically a world question, and is being considered in all of its phases by numbers of people interested in the world's development. In looking over the learning of this question, I have been amazed at the vast number of people learned in sociology and in science who insist that this is the only method of settling the destiny of the two races in America. I will be pardoned if I do not go into a close detail of the physical discussion. As Le Conte well says, there is no question but that the crossing of different varieties within the limits of the primary race may produce good effect, but that the crossing of the primary races themselves has been at all times and under all circumstances ruinous. Race aversion is the best evidence of the fact that the danger line has been passed. I mean race aversion in the scientific sense.

Of all the races, we presume that the farthest apart are the black-skinned Negro and the Teuton race, the latter to which we largely belong. These are extreme types, and their permanent union would be, in all probability, the worst of any union which could be devised as between nations. What we are trying to do is to save the Negro race as well as our own. It is in greater danger than the white race. In all countries and at all times the inexorable rule has been that the weaker race has been annihilated by the stronger. This has been especially the case in the all-rule of the Saxon race. We wish to preserve the Negro for some splendid characteristics with which he is endowed. That the

Negro has magnificent characteristics is shown by the fact that his is the only race which has ever risen from the iron rule of the Anglo-Saxon.   In every other case in conclusions with the Anglo-Saxon, the weaker race has been held by an iron hand, or has been wiped out of existence.   The Negro to-day is as strong as ever, notwithstanding his contention with this dominant race. It would not be fitting at this place to go into a discussion of the physical differences, but with two races in which there is the great difference in the grade of evolution that exists between the Anglo-Saxon and the Negro races, class distinction seems to be absolutely necessary for the preservation of both.   I will remark here at this point of the discussion that this race instinct exists not alone in the South, but it is as strong and vigorous in the North.   The obvious reasons of its acuteness in the South are the closeness of our contact with the Negroes, and the near knowledge of their overwhelming danger to the white race and to the country.

In proportion to the number of Negroes in the South, in proportion to their intelligence and to their effect upon the body politic, there is as much race instinct and race prejudice to-day in the North as there is in the South. Reflect but for a moment that there is 92 per cent. of the Negroes in the South ; that in Louisiana, Mississippi, and South Carolina more than one-half of the inhabitants are Negroes, and in South Carolina, three out of every five people whom you meet are Negroes.   In most places in the North only 1 per cent. are Negroes, and at the highest, 5 per cent. With this statement before us, let me ask our Northern friends, who suggest the idea of Assimilation as an easy escape from the Race Question, what are their feelings upon the initiative steps of this process? Of the intelligent Negroes of the North, how many places of public trust are held by them? To what offices are they elected? What part have they in the social organizations of the North? Do the hotels welcome them? Have they any place in the homes of the Northern men, and does the Northern man visit the Negro's home as a guest? As a matter of fact is not the prejudice in the North as great as it is in the South? And here let me say, in no spirit of recrimination, that in any State in the North, where large numbers of Negroes have been massed therein, the troubles have come more quickly and have been more deadly in their consequences than in the South. I am not pointing the finger of criticism at the Northern States, but am simply attempting by illustration to enforce this great doctrine of race integrity. Let us reason from a higher law than the mere physical law that we have been discussing. Let us appeal to the great destiny of the nation pushing its civilization over the earth, and let us find out from history what has been the effect of the amalgamation of two primary races so different as the Negro and the white man.

Canon Rawlinson, who has investigated this question to a greater extent than any man in this century, filled as he was with the idea of the amalgamation of the races, admits that, beyond any question, the settlement of the Race Question by this process in the United States is the most perplexing question which has ever come before the world for settlement.

Basing our intense opposition to this method upon precedent, we appeal to history to settle for the Southern race the question of the amalgamation of the races. I will be pardoned for a most apposite quotation from Dr. Palmer.

" 1. Before all the others there is the problem of race in adjusting the relationship between two distinct people that must occupy the same soil. It is idle to blink it, for it stares us in the face wherever we turn; and the timidity or sensitiveness which shrinks from its discussion is equally unwise and unsafe, for the country needs to know the comprehensive principles which will compel its settlement. Under the old régime, the relation between the two was exceedingly simple, because it was domestic. The bonds were those of guardianship and control on the one side, of dependence and service on the other. All this is now changed, and the two races are equal before the law. The suddenness of this translation, without any educational preparation for the new position, was a tremendous experiment. It furnishes an illustration of the heroic boldness of American legislation, and its early and successful solution will afford the most conspicuous proof of the vigor of the national life. My own conviction is, that it is a far too delicate and difficult problem to be solved by empirical legislation—either by the state on its political side, or by the Church on its ecclesiastical side. It must be patiently wrought out in the shape which an infinitely wise Providence shall direct — and it needs the element of time, with its silent but supreme assimilating and conciliatory influence. But so far as I can understand the teachings of history, there is one underlying principle which must control the question. It is indispensable that the purity of the race shall be preserved on either side; for it is the condition of life to the one, as much as to the other. The argument for this I base upon the declared policy of the Divine Administration from the days of Noah until now. The sacred writings clearly teach that, to prevent the amazing wickedness which brought upon the earth the purgation of the Deluge, God saw fit to break the human family into sections. He separated them by destroying the unity of speech; then by an actual dispersion, appointing the bounds of their habitations, to which they were conducted by the mysterious guidance of His will. The first pronounced insurrection against His supremacy was the attempt of Nimrod to oppose and defeat this policy; and the successive efforts of all the great kingdoms to achieve universal conquest have been but the continuation of that primary rebellion— always attended by the same overwhelming failure that marked the first. Among the methods of fixed separation between these original groups, was the discrimination effected by certain physical characteristics, so early introduced that no records of tradition or of stone assign their commencement, and so broadly marked in their respective types as to lead a class of physiologists to deny the unity of human origin. I certainly believe them to be mistaken in this conclusion, and firmly hold to the inspired testimony that 'God hath made of one blood all nations of men, for to dwell on all the face of the earth.' But there is no escape from the corresponding testimony, biblical and historical, that the human family, originally one, has been divided into certain large groups, for the purpose of being kept historically distinct. And all attempts, in every age of the world, and from whatever motives, whether of ambitious dominion or of an infidel humanitarianism, to force these together are identical in aim and parallel in guilt with the usurpation and insurrection of the first Nimrod.

"However true that the specific varieties within these groups may safely intermingle and cross each other, the record of four thousand years confirms the fact that there can be no large or permanent commixture of these great social zones without ruin ; and that ruin as complete as can be conceived, since it extends to the entire physical, intellectual, and moral nature. Follow the history of colonization by the Anglo-Saxon and Latin races respectively. The former, distinguished by what I may be permitted to term the instinct of race, has steadfastly refused to debase its blood by such a mixture ; and over all the world, in all latitudes, their colonies have thriven. England, for example, boasts to-day of her immense dependencies amidst the snows of Canada and the jungles of India. On the other hand, the latter, with a feebler pride of race, has blended with every people, and filled the earth with a mixed breed— the most emasculated to be found upon the globe, incapable of maintaining a stable government anywhere, or of developing the resources of the lands they burden with their presence."

Specifically let us see what has been the effect of the amalgamation upon the races.

Take for example the miserable inhabitants of West Griqualand of South Africa, hybrids of Dutch colonists and Hottentots, the Zambos of Western South America, mongrels of mixed European and the native Americans, the Portuguese-Malay half-castes of the East Indies, half-breeds of New Zealand, the Dutch-Malay half-breeds of Java, the Mongolian and Slavic amalgamation of Russian Asia, and the Portuguese and Negro population of Brazil. In every one of these instances, there is to-day a living horrible example of the mixing of the primary races. It is only necessary for me to mention these without further discussing them. They are treacherous, low in intelligence, wretched in body and physical make-up, unstable as the water, entirely unfit for governmental affairs, miserable, wretched hybrids. The most wonderful example we have today of the mixing of the races is in Egypt, where for ages the project of amalgamating the Negro and the Caucasian has been tried under the protection of the law, the Negro flowing in on one side and the Caucasian out on the other, thus furnishing the world's finest opportunity for the intermingling and commingling of the two primary races of the earth. Whenever the Caucasian would attempt to clear itself, it would be intermingled again by the influx of the Negro slaves. Is not Egypt a sufficient example of the ill effects of the philanthropic idea of some of our friends? A mongrel race without power or character, making a ruin of the land which for ages was the seat of the highest civilization on the face of the earth. The race never succeeded until it was put under the strong hand of the Anglo-Saxon. Is there need for fuller argument than we have before us in Mexico, South and Central America, and Hayti? Is it the time in the history of the world that the nation's life should be trifled with? The great problem of social and representative government has been settled by the Anglo-Saxon in this country. He has just levelled the forest, built the city, and opened the road. He has placed here the most magnificent civilization on the earth, founded, populated the state, levelled the mountain, and has destroyed all of the physical obstructions which have been before him. The vast spaces which the world considered could not be occupied for hundreds of years he has in one generation filled with smiling plenty and with the habitations of happiness and of pleasure. He will not stop here. His earth hunger is not appeased. He has settled largely the physical and governmental questions in this country. He has stepped across to the Islands of the Sea, and the hand of the Anglo-Saxon is to-day upon the East, from which he will not recede. He will no longer be satisfied with his own continent and his own people, and the Anglo-Saxon race to-day in the world is nerving itself practically for the world's conquest and a contest with all nations of the earth. "One hundred years hence," says Lavelaye, "there will be two colossal powers in the world, beside which Germany, England, France, and Italy will be as pigmies —the United States and Russia." I ask if, with this marvellous future before us, we shall risk this world-conquest by an ill-attempted settlement of the question by a race admixture which may arrest the race which seems to be destined by the Almighty for the civilization of the world? The risk is too great, and the discussion seems needless.

The only plan upon which the Negro can work out his destiny is along the lines of a separate race entity. That is a practical solution of the situation. He was for 150 years a chattel and a slave, dependent entirely upon his master for everything in life ; dependent for his clothes, for his medicine, for his shelter, and for his protection. Since the period of slavery was completed, he has been for over thirty years the ward of the nation. Millions of dollars have been poured out upon him. Help has been extended in every way. He was hedged about immediately after his emancipation by the victorious armies of the North. The Freedman's

Bureau, with its race of dependents, was in charge of affairs. For every morsel of food which went into his mouth, for every scrap of clothes upon his back, he was dependent upon the white race. To such an extent, in the first years of his emancipation, was this condition of dependence carried out, that to a great measure was destroyed his independence of character. Outside of the great Race Question, is the other great question, if the Negro expects to become a factor in the civilization of this day, he must not be a mere hanger-on to the white race. Not only race unity is absolutely necessary to him, but social race separation is as important. Mixed schools mean the white teacher in every instance; mixed churches mean the white preacher; mixed hotels mean the ownership of the property by the white man and the serving by the black man. In every instance, it means that the Negro, instead of having inculcated within him the idea of independence, of striking out for himself, of uplifting himself, will depend upon the stronger hand of the white man to guide him. Without confidence in himself, he can never become a potent factor in the civilization of this day. He can never become a missionary to other lands when he himself never preaches. He can never become a manager in the business of this day when he occupies a servile position to those who manage the affairs of to-day. As I have said before, over and above the great question of race instinct, the situation of to-day demands the absolute independence of the Negro in all of the race and social affairs of this life.

This is the question which now arises. If neither Diffusion, Colonization, nor Absorption will effect the purpose, what remedy do you propose? It seems to me that the best plan is to inaugurate the most efficient plan of industrial and general education for the Negro in all of the affairs of life, and in the meantime to restrict the suffrage to an intelligence or property basis, or a combination of both bases. The acute race troubles in the South have risen mainly from two causes, ignorance and politics. The ignorant use of his political powers has done more to keep the Negro and white man estranged than all other causes combined. There can be no practical solution of the question of the races in the South without settling the political question. When the Negro has arrived at an intelligence basis, absolutely the same to both the white and the black voter in the State in which he lives, then, and not until then, should he be entrusted with a vote. I will be excused for a discussion which is to some extent fundamental, and the discussion may seem contrary to the popular proposition that all men are free and equal. My time will allow but a glance at the general principles. It may seem to our friends in the North that we are presenting them with a club rather than an olive branch, but the doctrine that the government should be under the control of those best capable of self-government has been recognized at all times and, with one exception, under all circumstances, as being the true idea of proper government. Wherever this fundamental principle has been departed from, governmental ruin and personal loss have surely followed. It may be inquired, if this proposition is true, and if such is the view of the Southern people, why has it not been heretofore acted upon? We reply that no opportunity has been given the South. That those governing in the South previous to the abolition of slavery were substantially the best and the most intelligent of its people, but that the voting population which has been cast *en masse* upon the South since the war has been to an unheard of extent ignorant and injurious to the state. The survival of the fittest and the rule of the intelligent is a law which is as inexorable as any known to students in the science of government. Place two classes of people, one intelligent and the other ignorant, in the same country, and the intelligent element will surely govern. Place two races in the same country side by side and the superior or intelligent race will as surely dominate. The illustration of Le Conte is apposite. Place upon a desert island 100 children ten years old and 100 people in fair health, strength, and age. Surely those of adult age will govern and should govern the country according to their own ideas. Take his further proposition of 1000 Australian blacks on an island and 1000 educated Caucasians living with them. The whole salvation of the government of that territory depends upon the intelligent portion of the community controlling its affairs. I do not mean by this doctrine that the intelligent should enslave the weaker and less intelligent portion of the denizens of the country. You cannot argue a reasonable proposition to the *reductio ad absurdum*. The Negro in this country has the right of freedom and to the civil rights granted him by the law, and to all of the natural rights which the law and the constitution give him, but the highest and best law of self-preservation militates against the proposition that the greatest political rights of the country should be turned over to a class unfitted to exercise them. If this proposition is not carried out surely comes with it the destruction of the state. As an English statesman has said, the freeing of the blacks, the conferring upon them the franchise, was the boldest governmental experiment of modern times. The English government in all of its governing wisdom has held strictly the reins of government in its own hands in its dealings with the less intelligent races. In India, where the country swarms with a race which is certainly the equal of the Negro in intellectuality and governing capacity, the supreme rule is held tightly and closely by the English as the governing body. It is the true axiom of government that the higher or more intelligent class of people shall control. This has been the experience of 3000 years of governmental matters. In all of the history of government we have been the first people to abruptly modify this proposition. Left to the result of education alone after this great lapse of time possibly, the question may settle itself, but during that educational period, while the race is being enlightened and uplifted, governmental ruin would be the result.   We reason from the past to the future.   The Negro was not fitted for the reins of government.   When the government was turned over to him, he fell into the hands of men who, if they were not ignorant, were infinitely worse.   And you to whom I am talking have seen the effect of the violation of this fundamental rule.   The public debt in your State was increased from $8,000,000 to $25,000,000.   The debt of Tennessee was increased by $16,000,000; the debt of Georgia was increased $13,000,000.   In less than four months, North Carolina issued $25,000,000 of bonds for railroads.   The State debts in the South were increased nearly four hundred millions.   Martial law was proclaimed.   Every principle of the Magna Charta was thrown to the winds.   The sacred rights of *habeas corpus* were violated.   Negro regiments commanded by white renegades took men and women from their homes and incarcerated them in jail without warrant of law.   Men were returned for the highest offices in the land without the pretence of an election.   In the State of my birth, I have seen a judge on the bench who had never looked into a law book deciding questions of life and death.   I have seen a Negro clerk holding that important position when he could not sign his name to the records.   I have seen Negro officers sworn to protect the law when their whole official lives were engaged in protecting the lawbreaker and the scoundrel. Onerous laws were passed by the legislatures, honest debts were repudiated and dishonest ones created, personal liberty was ruthlessly violated, a reign of terror was witnessed throughout the length and breadth of the land. All of these evils came from the violation of the fundamental principle that the government of the state should be in the hands of the intelligent.

It is not my purpose to open old wounds or to bring back unpleasant memories or to stir up race animosities. It is my desire alone in the view I am taking to make the position of the Southern man plain and clear to the thinking world. The ignorant Negro is not properly qualified to cast a vote, and neither is the ignorant white man. As my distinguished friend, W. H. Baldwin, a Northern man, who more thoroughly than any one in the North whom I know understands this question, says: " When the Negro was freed under the constitution, he was given equal rights with the white citizens; suffrage was thrust upon him. This was injurious to him as well as to the white man. He was not ready for it, and he could not use it intelligently. From this cause alone the difficulties of the problem have been infinitely increased. How could we hope that it would be successful? After thirty-five years, we find the Negro practically disfranchised in many of the Southern States, and he should be if he is not properly qualified to cast a vote; but his qualifications should be determined in exactly the same manner as the qualifications of the white man ; and to this the Negro has no objection. The legal right of the Negro to vote has been the only serious cause of hostility on the part of the Southern white man. The Negro is the friend of the white man in all matters except politics ; but in politics he has seldom joined forces with his white neighbors for the common interest of the community in which he lives. If the time comes when the Negro is sufficiently educated, sufficiently intelligent to deal with political questions purely as questions relating to the community in which he lives, and without regard to sentimental party lines, he will receive more reasonable consideration from the whites in the South. Now is the time when he should recognize this opportunity.''

This is our great trouble. Under the constitution as it stands, ignorant numbers in many States give the right of control of the State government. This may be true as a matter of statute law, but it is against the great fundamental principle of the best government of the State and the preservation of the people, and wherever this principle meets the statute law of the land, the statute law will surely be broken to pieces. The higher law will always rule without regard to statutes and limitations.

Salus populi suprema est lex.

The political question has practically brought about

the acute trouble between the races. It has debauched the ballot-box and has terrorized both the white and the Negro. It is not alone debauching to the Negro but to the white man in the South. To allow the Negro the vote to which his numbers in many cases entitle him means the ruin of the State, and to take away from him that statute right means the violation of the laws of the land, a position the horrors of which should appeal to every man who loves his country and believes in perpetuating its institutions and keeping its laws unbroken. The South stands ready to give the Negro every right granted by the laws, but it exacts that as a condition the substantial political control of the State must be kept with the white man as the more intelligent. Then, how can this danger be eliminated without casting upon the disfranchised the odium such as usually applies to those generally excluded by the suffrage statute? How can we place the disfranchised so that with their own efforts they may become voters? The South desires the best interest of the Negroes, and desires to give them the franchise when they are sufficiently intelligent to properly use it. Thus, we are brought to the proposition that there is but one plan to enable us to be honest to the Negro, preserve the statute laws and at the same time save unharmed the great fundamental law of the preservation of the State. That is, to do away with the enforced debaucheries of the ballot, settle the question by inaugurating the highest and most efficient plan of education for the Negro and by confining the ballot to the intelligent citizen, white or black. If this is adopted, it should be carried out impartially and absolutely, and under this plan the interference with any intelligent voter, white or black, should be visited with the most rigorous penalties known to the law. The glory of the State would be in its intelligent voting population, and the disgrace and dishonor of the State would be in taking from any member of that intelligent voting citizenhood the right to cast his vote in any manner he may desire. The limiting the vote in this manner, I insist, should fall impartially upon the intelligent voter, whatever may be his color. The ignorant white voting population of the South is practically as dangerous to her institutions as the ignorant voter in the Negro ranks. Naturally, however, by reason of the greater number of Negroes in some sections, it would mean, and I frankly say it is intended to mean, the elimination of a great many ignorant Negroes from the franchise. I boldly say that this is the intention so to do, and the plan of my discussion here to-day is to eliminate the ignorant Negro voter until by education he is able to take an intelligent part in the government of the country. The taking away from the colored voter any part of the electorial franchise which, under the pre-existing state of affairs, belongs to him, carries with it the corresponding proposition that, under such a condition, the government of the State must absolutely assume the protection of the Negro. I am perfectly plain in saying that, whilst under the existing circumstances we have done well by the Negro, still the people of the South, worried, antagonized, and humiliated by the question of Negro control, have not had that regard for their own interests which they should have had in affording absolute and earnest protection to the Negro under all circumstances. The South is being injured by this class of crime, and it should be mercilessly stamped out. We have done well, I admit, under the circumstances, but it is our bounden duty to increase this protection in the future.

In order that what I may say may not appear treasonable, I will say that these views as to the restriction of the Negro vote to an intelligence basis were the views of the wisest men in the Emancipation era.

Mr. Lincoln in his letter to Governor Hahn says: "Now, you are about to have a convention which, among other things, will probably define the elective franchise. I barely suggest for your private consideration whether some of the colored people may not be allowed in, as for instance the very intelligent, and especially those who have fought gallantly in our ranks."

Mr. Sumner believed in Negro suffrage only for the reason that "their votes are needed in the North as well as at the South. There are Northern States where the good cause can be made safe by their votes beyond question. There are other States where the vote will be like the last preponderating weight in a nicely balanced scales. Let them vote in New York and the scales which hang so doubtful will incline toward the Republican cause."

Mr. Stevens, in February, 1867, and the President endeavored to carry out a plan by giving a suffrage to all male citizens who could read and write and owned $250 worth of property. In 1866, Mr. Stevens introduced a bill to reconstruct North Carolina upon a basis giving the franchise to males able to read and write. President Grant in his message, December 7, 1875, used the following language :

"Make education compulsory so as to deprive all persons who can not read and write from becoming voters after the year 1890, disfranchising none, however, on grounds of illiteracy who may be voters at the time this amendment takes effect."

President Johnson, in his veto of the District of Columbia Suffrage Bill, on January 5, 1867, uses the language, which is extremely appropriate to the subject under discussion : " Possessing these advantages but a limited time, the greater number, perhaps, having entered the District of Columbia during the latter years of the war, or since its termination, one may well pause to inquire whether after so brief a probation they are, as a class, capable of intelligent exercise of the right of suffrage and qualified to discharge the duties of official position. . . . Clothed with the elective franchise, their numbers, already in excess of the demand for labor, would soon increase by an influx from the adjoining States. Drawn from fields where employment is abundant, they would in vain seek it here, and so add to the embarrassment already experienced from the large class of idle persons congregated in the District. Hardly yet capable of forming correct judgments upon the important questions that often make the issues of a political contest, they could readily be made subservient to the purpose of designing persons. . . . It is within their power to come into the District in such numbers as to have supreme control of the white race and to govern them by their own officers, and by the exercise of all the municipal authority, among the rest, of the power of taxation over property in which they have no interest."

His statement was borne out by the fact that when Negro suffrage was found in the District of Columbia to be entirely and utterly out of keeping with the Negro's educational qualifications, the suffrage in the District of Columbia was wiped out by act of Congress.

The restriction of the ballot-box to the intelligence basis is not a new proposition in this country. In the North the idea first had its origin, and it has been successfully carried out. Connecticut in 1885, and Maine in 1892, adopted provisions of law limiting the suffrage to an intelligence basis, and a distinguished statesman of Rhode Island, in relating the restrictions placed upon the ignorant foreign vote, emulates the language of an orator from the "Black Belt" of the South. He says: "These men, thus transformed into American citizens in violation of the plainest provisions of law, ignorant of our institutions, unacquainted with our forms of government, embittered against all government, and ready with little solicitude to become the instruments of demagogues, are sufficiently dangerous when absorbed in the great agricultural States where healthy American sentiment pervades; but they are a menace to the public qualifications and the stability of legislation and orderly government when precipitated in overwhelming numbers upon a small country like Rhode Island."

In the South there have been various methods adopted for the suppression of the ignorant vote. They are summarized in the following : The payment of taxes before voting, centralizing the vote by the use of a number of ballot-boxes and the complication of the election laws, and recently by an express educational qualification. All of these systems, except the last, are vitally defective. This has been shown in practice. The great defect of all the Southern systems, except the educational basis, has been that the exercise of the ballot has no uplifting effect upon the Negro. The causing him to get rid of his tax receipts, the arrangement to centralize the vote and thus take from him that which the Negro thinks he has a right to, and the system of complicating the ballot-boxes, are all detrimental to the white as well as irritating to the Negro. There is no hope either for the white man or the Negro under such a system. It is hurtful to the whole body of voters, white and black, and every intelligent man in the South recognizes that as soon as possible both races should escape from the anomalous position in which they have been placed. The white man of the South desires to be fair. His object is to be honest with the Negro. It is only compulsion which makes him adopt any system which is unfair to the Negroes. In every State in which the intelligence basis has been adopted it has been successful. The elections have been orderly. The acute questions are eliminated. In Louisiana, in the by-election since the adoption of the intelligence basis, the elections have been quiet and orderly and entirely fair. In Mississippi and South Carolina, the Race Question has been largely eliminated. From every section of the State in which this basis has been adopted, there comes the report of the success in the practice of the statute confining the ballot to the intelligence basis. There is no intention to disfranchise the Negro as a class. It is not intended to violate the provision as to discrimination on account of the " race, color, or previous condition of servitude," but it is intended to do away with any questions as to the fairness of the elections in the South, and to place the highest exercise of citizenship in the hands of those best qualified to exercise its provisions. As the citizens of the country, white or black, become qualified, they should be and will be admitted absolutely impartially in the exercise of the ballot. From a somewhat intimate knowledge of the South and of the men who are in control of its affairs, I believe that there is no possible question but that the intelligent black will be allowed to approach the ballot-box and exercise his right to vote as impartially as the intelligent white man. The restriction of the ballot will do away largely with the acute issue.

It now remains in the line of our discussion to ascertain what has been done for the Negro in the way of education in the South, and what has been the effect of education upon the Negro, whether he has appreciably progressed by reason of that education in the direction of an intelligent voting citizenship. If you so restrict his ballot, will he ever become sufficiently intelligent? It has been somewhat the fashion among certain of our Northern friends to hold out the idea that it has been a half-hearted attempt upon the part of the South to educate the Negro, and that what has been done has been done largely through Northern philanthropy, and that the South has only been playing at public education. Let me say that the war left the South absolutely prostrated, farms devastated, homes destroyed, manufactories levelled, State and personal credit entirely gone through twelve years of actual battle and political debauchery. The South, rising from its stricken condition, undertook honestly and faithfully to educate her former slaves. I will be pardoned for a full discussion of the statistics applying to the education of the Negroes for the twofold purpose of showing the great increase of educational facilities in the South, and the intelligent appreciation of the education upon the part of the Negroes. The settlement of this question is crucial to our discussion.

In the slave-holding States in 1870-71, there was expended by the South $800,000 in round numbers for the education of the colored race. The expenditure per capita of the school population was $2.97 for the white and 49c. for the Negro. In 1872 and 1873, this sum had increased to practically $1,000,000 on the part of the South, with an increase to 54c. per capita for the colored population. Mark you, this was in a year when in my State a man who had carried a musket in the Southern army was not allowed either to vote or to hold office ; when the South had not yet risen from the ashes of her destroyed homes. In 1878, for the Negro, there was expended in the Southern States, in round numbers, $2,200,000, with an expenditure of $1.09 per capita for the colored race, double what it had been five years before. In 1886 and 1887, it had risen to the grand total of $4,500,000 for the education of the colored race, and $1.86 expenditure per capita for that race. In 1891 and 1892, it had risen to $5,500,000 for the colored race, or $2.15 per capita for the colored Southern school population. In 1897 and 1898, this sum had swollen to $6,600,000, in round numbers, with a per capita of expenditure for the colored school population, to $2.34. In absolute school expenditure in all these years, with the States rocking from the throes of a revolution such as the world has never seen, the Southern people of the

United States expended in round numbers $103,000,-
ooo for their former slaves. This statement will be
emphasized by the propositions that in Georgia the
Negroes in 1892 returned, in round numbers, $15,000,-
ooo of taxable property, against $450,000,000 returned
by the whites ; that in North Carolina, in 1891, there
was $234,000,000 worth of property listed for taxation
by the white people, as against only $8,000,000 for the
colored people, and in the State of South Carolina,
$1.81 is raised from each taxpayer to provide $1.00 for
each school child ; while in Montana only 36c. has to
be raised. I would think that the example of South-
Carolina alone would be an answer to any criticism on
the part of any section when you will understand that
two-thirds of the taxpayers in South Carolina are
colored, and they possess scarcely any property in the
State. In Virginia, in 1891, the tax collected from
white citizens amounted to $3,000,000 in round num-
bers, and from the colored citizens, $163,000. The
amount paid for public schools for the whites, $588,000,
and for the Negroes, $324,000. In all of the Southern
school systems there is no distinction against the
Negroes, except to say that there shall be separate
schools.

But pardon this digression from my main argument.
Let us by actual figures carefully consider the effect of
education upon the Negro. Is he approximating the intelligent voting citizen ? Says the School Commissioner
of the United States : " The enrollment of the colored

people was a little more than 27 per cent. of the full
enrollment in the Southern States, and they received
upwards of 20 per cent. of the money expended. As a
matter of fact, a comparatively small amount of this
was collected from the taxation of colored citizens." I
quote the able Commissioner: "The white people of the
South believed that the State should place a common-
school education within the reach of every child, and
they have done this much to give every citizen, white
and black, an even start in life." Now, continuing our
statement, has the Negro since the war increased his
intelligence to such an extent as to justify the argument that within a comparatively short time he will
become an intelligent citizen and win' an intelligent
as well as a legal right to citizenship? I again follow
the discussion of the intelligent Commissioner of Education. It is authoritative as well as careful. "In 1870,
more than 85 per cent. of the colored population of the
South over ten years of age could not read. In 1880 the
illiterate had been reduced to 75 per cent., and in 1890
to 60 per cent. of the colored population. In many of
the States of the South the percentage is even below 50.
In thirty years 40 per cent. of the illiteracy of the Negro
race had entirely disappeared.

"The total enrollment in the public schools of the
sixteen Southern States and the District of Columbia
for the year 1896-7 was 5,398,076, the number of colored children being 1,460,084 and the number of white
children 3,937,992. The estimated number of the chil-

dren in the South from five to eighteen years of age was 8,625,770. Of this number, 2,816,340, or 32.65 per cent., were children of the Negro race, and 5,809,430, or 67.35 per cent., were white children. It will be seen that the number of colored children enrolled was 51.84 per cent. of the colored school population, and the number of white children enrolled was 67.79 per cent. of the white school population. The average daily attendance in the public schools of the Southern States was 3,565,611, the number in the colored schools being 904,505, or 61.95 per cent. of the colored school enrollment, and the number in the average attendance in the white schools being 2,661,106, or 67.58 per cent. of the white school enrollment.

"It may be noted that in Louisiana, Mississippi, and South Carolina, the colored school population exceeds the white school population. In Kentucky, the number of colored children enrolled was 65.52 per cent. of the colored school population, a percentage of enrollment for the colored schools greater than in any other State, and larger than the percentage of white enrollment in at least six of the Southern States. In the colored schools of Alabama, Arkansas, Louisiana, and South Carolina, the average daily attendance was a greater percentage of their enrollment than was credited to the white schools of the same States upon their enrollment. Of the 119,893 public-school teachers in the Southern States, 27,435 belong to the colored race. There was one colored teacher to every 33 colored children in average attendance, and one white teacher to every 29 white children in average attendance.

" For the year 1896–7, the total expenditure for the public schools of the sixteen Southern States and the District of Columbia was $31,144,801. The cost of the schools for the colored race can not be accurately stated, but a fair estimate will place the cost of the colored schools at about $6,575,000. This is something over 20 per cent. of the aggregate expenditure of the Southern States, while the average attendance of colored children was about 26 per cent. of the entire average attendance of white and colored pupils.

" There are at least 178 schools in the United States for the secondary and higher education of colored youth exclusively. Of this number, one was in Illinois, two in Indiana, one in New Jersey, two in Ohio, and three in Pennsylvania, the remaining 169 being in the Southern States.

" In the 169 schools, there were employed 1795 professors and teachers, 787 males and 1008 females. There was a total enrollment in these schools of 45,402 students, 20,243 males and 25,159 females, an increase of 5275 over the enrollment of the previous year. In collegiate grades there were 2108 students, 1526 males and 582 females, an increase of 653 over the previous year. In the secondary grades there were 15,203 students, 6944 males and 8259 females, an increase of 1640 over the year before. In the elementary grades of these secondary and collegiate institutions, there were 28,091 pupils, 11,773 males and 16,318 females, an increase of 2999 over the year 1895–6.

" In all the colored schools there were 2410 students pursuing the classical course, 1312 males and 1098 females. There were 974 students in scientific courses, 447 males and 527 females. In English courses there were 11,340 students. The business courses had 295 students, 179 males and 116 females. There were 5081 students in normal or teachers' training courses, 2382 males and 2699 females. There were 117 graduates from college courses, 103 males and 14 females. There were 1256 graduates from normal courses, 537 males and 719 females. The high-school courses had 846 graduates, 333 males and 513 females. In all there were 1311 professional students, 1137 males and 174 females. There were 611 students and 68 graduates in theology, 104 students and 30 graduates in law, 345 students and 71 graduates in medicine, 38 students and 10 graduates in dentistry, 39 students and 20 graduates in pharmacy and 174 students and 35 graduates in nurse training.

" That in the 169 schools for the colored race there were 13,581 pupils and students receiving industrial training, 4970 males and 8611 females. The number in industrial training was almost 40 per cent. of the total enrollment in these schools. There were 1027 of these pupils being trained in farm and garden work, 1496 in carpentry, 166 in bricklaying, 144 in plastering, 149 in painting, 85 in tin and sheet-metal work,

227 in forging, 248 in machine shops, 185 in shoemaking, 689 in printing, 6728 in sewing, 2349 in cooking, and 2753 in other trades. In the libraries of these schools there were 244,794 volumes, valued at $203,731. The aggregate value of grounds, buildings, furniture, and scientific apparatus was $7,714,908. The value of benefactions or bequests received during the year 1896–7 was $303,050. The schools received from the public funds for support for the year $271,839, from tuition fees $141,262, from productive funds $92,080, and from sources not named $540,097, making an aggregate income of $1,045,278 for the year."

These figures are tiresome, but they teach one of the greatest lessons of the century. In the line of this argument, the valuable statistics of the Commissioner of Education showed that in 1890, the Negroes occupied 550,000 farms; of the number of homes in the country 900,000 were occupied by the Negroes; that twenty-two per cent. of their farms were owned by the occupants, and that of the farms owned by the Negroes over ninety per cent. were without incumbrance. This shows a very safe and gratifying progress. This is not entirely a clear picture, and the bare figures may be somewhat optimistic. It will not be expected that the Negro will be educated within a few years. His education has been attended with great difficulties, and dis-couragements have been in every step in his existence. He has been a slave, has been degraded, and he lives in large masses which are dense and hard to reach. He has even now a comparatively small idea of economic conditions, and the burden of lifting him has been a tremendous one, but, in the judgment of those who have studied the question, he is now moving in the right direction, and this of itself speaks volumes.

In one view, a great deal has been done for the Negro. Large sums of money have been spent upon his education, yet a vast deal of this money has been poorly spent. People in the North, without the knowledge of the social and educational conditions in the South, have spent large sums of money in endowing sectarian and higher institutions for the Negro. They have lavished great sums of money in many instances on the education of the Negro for the professions of the law, medicine, politics, and the higher education. As a matter of fact, a great deal of this education has been entirely inopportune and misplaced. The Negro lawyer is almost entirely without clients. The Negro doctor is almost surely without patients; the Negro politician is a disturber to the country, and in vast numbers of instances the product of these institutions has been an injury to his race and the section in which he lives. There has been no disguising this proposition. Many of the institutions in their teachings have been narrow, and, as a matter of fact, it has been the experience of the Southern people that oftentimes their teachings have been an injury rather than a good to the Negro race. What the South wishes is to have the Negro educated thoroughly in body, soul, and mind. Let him become a useful farmer; let an effort be made to make a useful artisan; let him be taught the social economics of life, social ethics, how to live the cheapest and best; let him be taught the arts of bread-winning, and, instead of being a disturber, instead of being a useless hanger-on in the section in which he lives, he will be a builder-up of that section and an honor to his race. Do not understand me to decry special literary education. I am earnestly in favor of it. I think he should be educated, but, as a matter of fact, I do not believe he should be educated for pursuits which in the condition of affairs in this generation are practically closed to him. The new theory of industrial education is a most magnificent one, and I look in the next twenty years for a wonderful increase in the character, standing, and well-being of the Negro derived from this common-sense method of teaching. If the Northern philanthropist, instead of putting a few dollars in the special sectarian, political, or professional education of the Negro in some university in the South, would allow that money to be placed under the control of people who will, in connection with the Southern States, inaugurate a comprehensive, systematic, and general plan for the education of the Negro in the pursuits of life, a step will have been taken in the settlement of this question. This will be more effective than a dozen half endowed, half-officered universities teaching along their own lines without regard to a general system or under a general control. Many of these institutions in the same community are continuously going over the same ground as the neighboring school. A central board composed of first-class men of the North and of the South, full of the needs of the Negro in the South, would do more good in one year in dispensing Northern philanthropy among the Negroes than a dozen law, medicine, religious, or higher educational universities, each working in an aimless fashion. A busy, intelligent, and successful bread-winner, whether white or black, will be respected, and he will do more to bring about a settling of the great problem than a hundred briefless lawyers or doctors without clients or bookkeepers who can have no business.

Do not understand me to say that the general and industrial training, and the restriction of the ballot to a full intelligence or property basis, will entirely do away with the Race Question. I mean that when the naturally acute feelings which have been raised by the unintelligent exercise of the ballot by the Negro shall have been dissipated and he shall have become educated as an intelligent workman, the Race Question will be infinitely nearer solution. That is the practical aim of my discussion here to-day. It is entirely practical.

While the fields will take vast numbers of Negroes, the fields will no longer furnish them with employment. The household cannot in the future be relied upon to furnish them all with a supply of labor. They cannot be confined to the lower and heavier classes of labor.

Vast numbers of the Negroes must find employment in the higher classes of labor in the South. I believe that with the consummation of the industrial education inaugurated by General Armstrong at Hampton, and by Booker Washington at Tuskegee, that we will see a wonderful change in the Negro. In the South the labor lines are not so closely drawn as in the North, and they are daily lessening in their severity. If the Negro is made a fine artisan, either in the field or upon the wall or in the mill or at the bench, almost surely will he have work. One great injury to the Negro race is that there has not been sufficient employment for him. The consequence naturally is crime. This would be the consequence to either white or black not employed. This state of affairs cannot be continued by the South. The Negro must have work and the South must give it to him. We must look that situation squarely in the face. Even if the employment of the Negro in the trades and mills will lessen somewhat the price of labor, this must be one of the burdens of the South. This is a very plain statement, but it is true. That being the case, it will be better and easier for the South to give work to the intelligent workman, skilled in his trade and able to make his living, than to an ignorant one. Individuals must suffer in every great social or economic livelihood. It will be infinitely cheaper for the South to push this system of education all over the land for the Negro, than to support him in idleness and vice. He must be prepared for a higher class of labor. I repeat, the present class of labor is not sufficient for him. In this educational idea we must not deal in dreams. I insist that we shall not tell the Negro that his hope of standing in the South at the ballot and at work is dependent upon his labor; and then take the labor away from him. We must give him a chance, and I am glad to say that over the South is a desire to give the intelligent Negro all the chance he needs. I do not believe that educating the Negro as an artisan will affect the white man as has been expected in some quarters. Many people have informed me that the Negro coming into the intelligent field of labor in the future will intensify the Race Question. It may do so in isolated instances. Under a settled state of affairs, with the demand for labor at a minimum, it might cause serious trouble. In ordinary state of affairs in a settled community, such as the manufacturing communities in the North, where, if anything, manufacturing is lessening, or where just so much manufacturing is done, this might be the case; but in the South, where the mills and manufactories within the last ten years have been multiplied to an unprecedented extent, where labor is needed as it never was before, there will be no question but that the intelligent Negro artisan will be in demand. Every intelligent workingman in the South can make a living. We of the South who understand the vast possibilities of the South scarcely appreciate what we have done and what we are doing. We have been so engaged in building the South from its desolation that we have scarcely understood what an advance it has made in the commercial and manufacturing affairs of the world. It is only by comparison that we can see the wonderful opportunities for absorbing every particle of intelligent labor in the South. This commercial increase came slowly, but to-day it is increasing in arithmetical progression.

I will be pardoned if I give some plain figures of comparison made by Mr. Richard Edmonds, the greatest living master of Southern commercial conditions. The mere statement will enable us to appreciate the advance of the South and its marvellous growing ability to absorb all labor.

THE SOUTH—YESTERDAY AND TO-DAY.

	1880.	1899.
Railroad mileage	20,600	50,000
Cotton crops, bales	5,750,000	11,199,000
Cotton consumption in Southern mills, bales	233,006	1,231,000
Capital invested in Southern manufacturing	$257,200,000	$1,000,000,000
Grain produced, bushels	431,000,000	736,600,000
Value of Southern mfg. products,	$457,400,000	$1,500,000,000
Wages paid to factory hands in South	$75,000,000	$350,000,000
Capital invested in cotton-seed-oil manufacturing	$3,500,000	$40,000,000
Pig-iron produced, tons	397,000	2,500,000
Coal mined, tons	6,000,000	40,000,000

As a distinguished editor in the South well says, the increased prosperity that would come to the South could her idle Negroes be put to work would make place on a higher plane of employment for millions of white men.

I will say here that, as a matter of fact, whilst much has been done for the Negro, much of it has been badly done. For ten or fifteen years after his emancipation, he was largely in the hands of people who were using him for political effect. He was in a period of transition. He was disturbed in body and mind, his whole environment had been changed, and, I think, considering the vast disadvantages under which he has worked, that we see in him a bright hope that he will be uplifted and upbuilt, and become a useful, practical, and necessary member of the body politic. Dr. Mayo and Dr. Curry are the greatest of authorities upon this work, and Dr. Curry well says : "Of the desire of the colored people for education the proof is conclusive, of their capacity to receive mental color there is not the shadow of a reason to support an adverse hypothesis."

Dr. Mayo arrives at the same conclusion.

In conclusion, I will say that the problem will be worked out by the South. Wise men believe that the greatest danger is over. It seems the boundary limit has been passed. There is no question but that the races are greatly improved by daily contact with each other. There is a kindly feeling on both sides in all of the interests of life which are not racial and inherent. The racial distinction will be and should be permanent. In the business relations there is no question about a vast improvement and a desire on the part of each race to live and to let live. Each race is beginning to learn the true status of separate and race livelihood. Each race is beginning to understand that there are inherent and social antagonisms which cannot be over-stepped. This makes a vast advance. When this has been understood the relationship has been in every way improved. In addition to this our Northern friends no longer concern themselves with interfering with social affairs between the two races in the South. They understand that these matters the South will settle for herself. From the situation she is better able to settle them. This is redounding to the better relations of the two races. The idea of non-interference with the social status of the South will be vigorously insisted upon by the South, and this is being under-stood thoroughly in the North. I would be bold and arrogant and indeed foolish did I presumptuously suggest the plan which I have outlined as the only solution of the Race Question. Any man may seem presumptuous when he discusses the future of the Negro Question. With the lights before me it seems in the present state of evolution the most feasible plan. I do, however, know this with all my heart, that the education of the Negro, the making him better and more intelligent, and withholding the ballot from him until he has evolved himself into an intelligent citizen, is certainly the best plan for the present. Without look-ing into the future we know what is best for the present.

This plan seems less attended with difficulties than any other. With this general idea it will take years of patience and mutual forbearance. This is the greatest social question which has confronted any nation, and will not be settled without much travail, without many discouragements, and only by a long process of time. Neither the white man nor the negro is perfect, but I earnestly believe that the evolution of this great question and its full and complete settlement under the Providence of God will come in its own time and will conclude to the ultimate glory of our country.

III

THE ATTITUDE OF THE PROGRESSIVE SOUTH

W HEN your courteous note of invitation to address this splendid assembly of workers for
our country came to my home in the South,
my first impulse, after making full obeisance to you, was
to continue in the shadow of my mountains as one not
fitted by education or opportunity to discuss commerce
with the Masters of Trade. Yet, sir, the significance of
the event hurried my memory to other days long past,
and whispered that in this day of coming change no good
man, however humble, should turn his face away from
the rising sun or withhold his hand from the plough. The
son of a Southern soldier conferring with the men of the
North as to what is best for the Republic, with naught of
unkindness for the North, with naught of selfishness for
the South, but only with love and kindness for each,
and the welfare of the Republic crowning and glorifying all, fills me with emotions too sacred for expression,
and well assures me that, amidst the grave imaginings
of harm and hurtful change, the Republic is founded on
eternal foundations and that its glory and permanence
are secure. Ah, sir, when citizens hold before my eyes

that which they anxiously believe to be the hem of the Imperial Robe, my mind, for its inspiration for steady belief in the Republic, flies swiftly back to Old Virginia, my boyhood home. There rise before me the Blue Mountains of the Great Valley, crowned with the autumn sunlight and reflecting from their broad shoulders their kaleidoscopic glory of orange and green and flame over hill, river, and town.

Sir, it is God's own footstool. Amidst its mountains and in its valleys live a high-spirited people who have always prized liberty above other blessings. They are God-fearing, and from the mountain cliffs and the shades of the valley the evening prayer arises from happy homes, and only Freedom's call to arms can stop their songs of praise. It is a land of fatness, of rich meadow, of noble homes, with schools and colleges to crown the work.

Yet, on this beautiful day, there is no fatness in the land. The sun falls lovingly on the broad, winding river and beautiful valley, but the homes are blackened desolations, and from their sightless windows and broken walls stare want and grisly despair. The torch has marked its fiery way across the broad valley, and the smoking ruins are the sentinels standing guard over the desolate fields. The schoolhouses and colleges have disappeared with the homes, and the government is in the hands of aliens. The widow's weeds cast a shadow over every household, and the cry of the fatherless is as frequent as the whispering of the winds.

The little mounds are in every valley and on every hill-side, and the Gods of the Household, with sighs and sobbings, covering their sorrowing eyes, have taken flight to happier scenes.

On this far away autumn day in the South, after the war, was the real danger time to the Republic. If the South, in despair and insidious hate, more dangerous to the Republic than its armed legions, had permanently fallen away from its love of its traditions of the Republic, and had instilled this feeling in the hearts of the coming generation, surely within time we would have seen the disintegration of this government. Sir, it did not. On the day when in the little town nestling in the mountains we buried Robert E. Lee, we turned our faces towards the open day and gave our lives and our souls towards re-creating the broken homes, building up the desolated places, and tying together with hearts of love this great republican government. Then, Mr. Chairman, if the South can forget her woes and sorrows and desolation, and if the North and South, casting behind them the old days and the old enmities, can, in one short life, heal up the last trace of the greatest conflict the world ever witnessed, how idle does it appear to me, how infinitely idle, to see the destruction of free government and the ruin of the nation in the enlarging of our commerce and the extending of the civilization of our Republic !

The times are changing, must change. The isolation which is not alone the result of the policy inaugurated by the Fathers, but caused rather by the close local attention demanded by the development of our own country, cannot continue to be the policy most beneficial to our people. There has been heretofore no need to look over the sea into foreign lands for employment for our busy hands. Our rich mines heretofore have waited only for the touch of the pick to pour their golden flood into the lap of him who took for the finding. The rich and bounteous lands of the South and West are no longer waiting for the coming of the husbandman to bless him with their fatness and crown him with their glory of waving grain kissed into ripeness by the soft sun of our blessed land. Where but a generation ago there was the solitude of the prairie land, to-day the household gods watch over the fortunes of myriads of happy people. The prattle of children at play and the laugh of the contented workman as he drives the flying shuttle to and fro, weaving into the web and woof of his life his love of country, is heard where but the span of a short life was the lair of the wild beast and the sporting place of the wilder man. At the ocean side, on the rich plain, by the river, and under the mountain, are all the tremendous forces of the Republic at their mighty work. New conditions are arising, and necessarily should arise, under the powerful demands of a virile people, strengthened by the potent influence of the most progressive civilization which has been known to mankind. The policy of isolation, political and mercantile, died with the white sails of the ship, the filling of the prairie with homes, and by the production created by the energy of nearly a hundred millions of people at work. It died when the South turned the quiet fields into the manufactory and its villages into bustling cities. Its requiem was sung by the hurrying locomotive, the whispering telephone, the whirling propeller of the steamship, by the crowded manufactory which in six months' work can furnish sufficient for the needs of the whole year, by the grand contest between the civilizations of the East and the West, and above all by the Macedonian cry of the peoples of the earth, "come over and help us."

To those who see Roman triumphs and the flowing purple of the Imperial Robe in the widening of our commercial power to other lands and the extension of our civilization to broader fields, we simply answer that the immortal Virginian who penned the code of free government, when he added to our domain the mighty Louisiana land, was impeached in high places for casting the shadow of the Imperial Eagle over the land and giving the liberties of the people to its cruel beak. The little fringe along the Atlantic has added the flood of the Mississippi, the Missouri, and the Oregon to its domain. The will-o'-the-wisp and the glowworm light our flag at night under the palms of Florida, and by day its folds are touched by the sweet airs ladened with the incense of the orange and magnolia. Our Constitution is the highest law to the people of the Pacific, and from the banks of the Potomac they receive its highest interpretation. Yet, notwithstanding this glory of added domain, the Constitution has not been wrenched, nor has its rich inheritance of freedom been invaded. The glory of the Lord has surely been about and around this people. Here are the most exalted civilization, the purest Christianity, the most advanced science, the most absolute civil freedom which the world ever saw. The conditions are happier for us than they are for any other people. Justice is not bought or sold, nor held by the strong, but is for the rich and the poor. The citizen, enlightened and upheld by the genius of his country, is his own ruler, and in that no man can gainsay him. The workman, however humble, is a king in his own house, and only to the law of the land does he owe any allegiance.

But are these great blessings for us alone? Shall Ethiopia in vain stretch out her arms to us, and shall we turn away from the people in the shadows of the forests? Shall we not give as well as receive? Shall we remain at home and invite the rigid conditions, social and industrial, which inevitably come to a people living within itself? The most convincing argument that the great Instrument was made for broad conditions is that, although the domain under its provisions has widened and increased beyond the dreams of those who sat at its birth, yet still it has easily met every condition, and under its power seventy millions of people dwell in happiness and peace. In dwarfing that great instrument, in minimizing its wide provisions, in restricting and narrowing its interpretations so as to correspond with the horizon of some of them who affect to be entirely guided by its provisions, lies the conservatism which will work more real harm to the world and to the people than the radicalism so much appealed to and so lavishly criticised. The excess of conservatism is more to be feared than the radicalism, for the good common sense of the American people will sternly repress any radicalism which really threatens the permanence of our institutions. When by the fortunes of war or by honest purchase, new lands and people become subject to its provisions, surely we can give them the freedom, the liberal institutions, and the local self-government guaranteed to us by our Constitution. I appreciate, sir, that I have been late in announcing the specific text of my discussion. Appreciating that the question of greatest importance to-day is the question of Foreign Trade and Foreign Markets, it seems to me that it is of peculiar interest to you to know the position of the South upon this important question. It would not be becoming on this occasion for me to occupy your time with any matter of detail, and I will only attempt to generally indicate to you the position of the progressive South on the great questions which are to-day paramount in the commercial affairs of the American people. I take much pleasure in presenting a few suggestions for thought on the lines of—

The Attitude of the Progressive South towards the Measures for promoting the Country's Foreign Trade ; what the Country, and especially the North, will gain from the South's aid in making these Measures effective; and what the South is to expect in return for such aid.

The first question of absolute importance to-day to the North is the matter of the foreign markets. It is supreme in its importance to the whole people. We cannot longer live within ourselves, and such is the situation that, if the American people propose to assume their required position in the great foreign trade, they must grasp these markets. In a short time the opportunity will be lost, and our civilization will be restricted and our productive powers must be lessened.

Where are the markets which are necessary to this country's commercial progress, and what is the position of the South as to obtaining and holding them? First, of critical importance is the market of the Empire of China. This is the market for which Russia, Germany, Britain, and France, with all of their energies, are contending. Here is the most important market of the globe, and a market of peculiar importance to us in that it needs about everything we manufacture. Here are three hundred and fifty millions of people who have just begun their development of civilization and trade. To-day, without organized effort, we sell them twenty-five million dollars per year, and within a short time we will make it seventy-five million dollars. That means much to you. The mind can scarcely comprehend our interests in this trade when we consider our opportunities in an empire of four million square miles, inhabited by an energetic people just opening their eyes to civilization. There is scarcely an article which you manufacture in Newark which cannot be sold in China. Think for a moment of an empire of this vast extent with less than four hundred miles of railroad. You have more than that amount in the city of Newark. In the matter of rail-road building, we can undersell any other country. As an illustration of the opportunities of trade, they are to-day arranging to construct twenty thousand miles of railroad which will cost four hundred millions of dollars, and a vast part of this work should be in the hands of this country. Great cities are being built in Northern China. Here are the termini of the longest line of railroad in the world. Within a short time in this new territory, the American locomotive has under-sold those of every other country, and this year China has purchased from you and the South about eleven millions of dollars of cotton. Here are fast developing the great cotton markets of the world. These peo-ple need everything we manufacture. Already we have built up a great trade in cottons, machinery, leather goods, electric goods, chemicals, railroad equipment, tools, hardware, and the general products of our workshops. At the present rate of progress, our trade with China will, in fifteen years, be the most important of any trade in the world. With the short time at my disposal, it would be impossible to discuss it specifically. Here, sir, within twenty-five years, will be the world's field of trade. We deal with China through treaty rights, and these treaty rights are in jeopardy. To-day the mercantile nations of the world, Russia, Germany, England, and France, appreciating the marvellous possibilities of this great country, have established zones of control, which practically means that the United States, if she desires the markets of China, must come hat in hand and take the crumbs which fall from the table. I will add that from the table of the Lion, the Bear, and the Eagle fall but few crumbs. Under the vigorous policy of the State Department, arrangements, which are practically temporary, have been effected by which the door is not yet closed to us. We demand a vigorous policy which will be permanent in its effect, under which the rights of this country shall be preserved and under which the markets of China shall not be turned over to European nations as their own exclusive property, but shall be held alike on terms of absolute equality for the citizens of the United States. In this demand the South is urgent and insistent, and her greatest manufacturing organization has just demanded that the trade door of

China should be kept wide open to the markets of the world.

Now, sir, we are face to face with the great question, How shall we keep open to our country the door of the great Chinese and Eastern market? There is but one door for us and that is through the Philippine Islands. Here is the real strategical and commercial position of the East. Every Eastern market can be reached far more easily through these islands than from any other position. Shanghai and Hongkong, through which cities England has established her great trade, offer no such position for commercial success as do the Philippines. It gives control of the great northern and central coast of China, with its teeming, active population. It puts us in a position to grasp through them the markets of Japan with its forty millions of energetic people and its annual foreign trade of two hundred and fifty million dollars. The great coast line of the Philippine Islands of eight hundred miles practically dominates the northern coast of China, capable of a foreign trade of a billion dollars per year. We have less than ten per cent. of the Eastern trade, which amounts to two billion dollars per year, and our possibilities are apparent to every one. On this coast to-day are the greatest commercial activities extant. Manila can easily become, and will become, the distributing centre of the Eastern world. Here every commercial condition is at its best. Within a radius of twenty-five hundred miles we reach every great trade centre in the East and Australia. From this broad harbor our country will be mistress of the Eastern civilization as she is of the Western. In the islands for a century to come there is a field for the restless energies of our people, which, in our own country, will soon be denied to them. The foreign trade of these islands, which is now about thirty-five millions, under the vigorous vitalization of our people, will, according to the best experts, amount in five years to one hundred and fifty millions. In these islands abound the products needed for mankind, and it is the richest undeveloped territory yet remaining on earth. Holding no position in the East but that of a country having a treaty with an empire whose dismemberment has begun, our victory at Manila and the subsequent treaty gave to us a political and commercial position in the East which has heretofore been denied us. It prevented the dismemberment of the Empire of China, and it has given us the right of an open door to her markets. Without our position in the Philippines our commercial treaties with China would be valueless, and upon our withdrawal from those islands the Chinese Empire would not last a month, and its rich market would be forever lost to the people of this country. Without obtruding a political discussion upon this occasion, I say, very frankly, for I am used to plain speech, that, whatever may be the views of party, the commercial and business people of this nation have no intention of turning over this last great commercial Gibraltar to the Imperial Eagle of Germany which so impatiently awaits it.

The real sentiment of the people is illustrated by what occurred in my home last month. The son of a Southern soldier, a man of my name and blood, limped into my home with a Filipino bullet in his thigh. When I discussed with him the question of our giving up possession and control of the Philippines he significantly remarked, "The United States has never yet given up that for which she has fought, and certainly never that for which she has both fought and paid." I do not understand that our maintaining a commercial and political interest in these islands is incompatible with the fullest freedom for its inhabitants. Many who oppose our retaining any interest in these islands seem to imply that our retention of them is for the purpose alone of establishing a tyranny over the inhabitants. I find that thoughtful men are in favor of establishing the jurisdiction of our government, giving the Filipinos full control of their local affairs when they are able to manage them, and allowing them the highest measure of liberty, such liberty as they have never enjoyed, and such as they will not enjoy if our flag should be removed therefrom. To leave the islands is to turn them over to anarchy or to the German Imperial Government. Neither one of these conditions will be contemplated by the American people. Our people will work out the question according to good sense and in such manner as will give the Filipinos the fullest liberty and yet retain for our government such political and commercial powers as will allow us to control the trade of the Pacific and the Far East and forever hold the great door of China wide open so that through its majestic portals will flow into the East the religion, the arts, and the genius of the newest and best civilization which has ever blessed mankind.

Now, as to the position of the South on this last great question. What have been her traditions? Those who suggest that the South has been ultra-conservative as to the widening of the sphere of this country's influence do not know her traditions. As to her action in the future, I confidently refer you to her past. It would be but trite for me to say that the acquisition of our additional domain, excepting Alaska, was all by the practically solid vote of the South, and excepting the acquisition of Texas, under President Filmore, it was all acquired under the presidency of Southern men. In 1809 and 1810, Mr. Jefferson and Mr. Madison, both men of the South, began the movement for the acquisition of Cuba and its incorporation into this government, and such was the settled and persistent policy of the South as long as she had influence in public affairs. As to the position of the progressive South, it is voiced by the Southern Cotton Spinners' Association, which demands in vigorous terms the closing of the Philippine question, in order that its markets and the markets of China may be fully open to our trade and commerce.

However rich and magnificent these markets may be, if a competitor has cheaper access thereto you receive no benefit.   Of the great Far East market I have just spoken.   There is another market which next to China is most important to us to control, that is the market of South and Central America.   In the Far East and in South and Central America five hundred millions of people are waiting for the products of our abundant energy.   Corea, Siam, China, the Philippine Islands, Japan, South America, and the Islands of the Sea desire your merchandise ; and these markets must be reached by a cheaper route than around Cape Horn. England, by the completion of the Suez Canal, has the advantage in trade routes.   Within twenty years, by the building of that canal, she has doubled her commerce to the East.

The building of the Nicaraguan Canal will be of infinitely more advantage to the American people than the Suez Canal has been to the British.   It will place each of these great markets nearer to your manufactories than they are to Liverpool or London.   With this canal completed, you can grasp in your strong hands the splendid markets of Central America and Western South America, and no one can compete therein with you.   The American manufacturer can turn out his product, man for man, cheaper than can the English, and thus, with shorter distance to the markets, you have the advantage over England.   Between London and Canton, the Suez Canal saves you three thousand three hundred miles, while the Nicaraguan Canal saves you from five to eight thousand miles on every voyage. Between London and San Francisco it saves only seven thousand miles, whilst between Newark and San Francisco it saves ten thousand miles out of a total of fourteen thousand eight hundred. With the canal completed, you will be seven thousand miles nearer to the rich markets of Western South America than you are to-day, and have that much advantage over Britain and your European competitors. Observe the trade to China, which is worth twenty-five millions of dollars. To make this voyage, it takes one hundred and seventy days by sail. By the canal, it will take less than one hundred days by sail and less than forty days by steam. Reverse the condition which the Suez Canal gives England, and your peerless shoes, your splendid machinery, your locomotives and cars, your iron and steel, your pottery, your cotton and woollen goods, and the thousands of products of your manufactories would, to a large extent, occupy the place of England's products. From Newark to Melbourne, it is, by Cape Horn, thirteen thousand five hundred miles; by the canal it is ten thousand miles, a saving of three thousand five hundred miles. It will give us the advantage over England in distance to the Japanese market. It will place us nearer to Northern China than will be our great rival. If, with a long voyage, we have made the vast strides in China's trade, which excited the surprise of Lord Beresford, the British

Commissioner to China, with all of the added advantages of distance with us, how long would it be until you could practically have the whole advantage in that great market? If the canal would cost you two hundred millions of dollars, it would increase our trade with our Western coast twenty-five million dollars at once. The lowest estimate would give us an equal amount per year with Western South America. In addition to these markets, here will be the opportunity to stand face to face with five hundred millions of people who want our products, and in every case we would have the advantage of distance over England. Was there ever such an opportunity for trade? Shall we grasp our opportunities and take our future within our own hands and practically control the trade of the Far East and South? It will increase our output and add to our factories. It will give a trade which will grow as your knowledge of the markets grow, and, as the people of the world become acquainted with your products, it will open the shipyards and will send the American sailors to every market of the universe. In this great question of such vital interest to you, what is the position of the South? I reply that the father of the Canal legislation, who for years has stood sponsor for this great work, is a Southern Senator; and in Congress, the vote of the South, with her whole influence, is being solidly exerted to complete this great work. The South has never faltered and no interest has ever interfered with her persistent desire to see this great work completed by

American hands and for the glory of American commerce.

To successfully carry out these great policies and control these markets we must have our own merchant marine. With our vast preponderance in manufacturing and productive ability it is a sad commentary upon the mercantile laws of the land which give to England, our great rival, the practical carrying trade of the world. The merchant marine is as important to our country as the manufacturing interest. No country can become a great carrying power unless it is a great ship-building country ; and no country can control the markets of the world unless it commands the means of reaching those markets. The immense sum which we pay year by year to foreign carriers should, by liberal laws in the future, be paid to our own people. The presence of the distinguished Chairman of the Committee on Commerce in the House of Representatives, who is to follow me, will not allow a prolonged discussion of this great question by me. As to the South, I only wish to add that she is earnestly in favor of liberal laws which will increase the American merchant marine. Many of you are in favor of the subsidy idea. Some of our progressive Southern people are in favor of discriminating duties. My want of familiarity with the subject will not allow me to say what is the best policy for our country to adopt in order that we shall have a merchant marine commensurate with our great commercial interests. In the South we are in favor of some liberal maritime policy which will allow us the influence in the commercial markets of the world which is called for by our great interests. We must control our carrying trade, and the progressive South will join earnestly in any fair policy which will encourage our again becoming a great ship-owning, ship-building, and carrying power. It is an anomaly in commerce to attempt to take away the markets from England and use English ships to accomplish the result.

Another and most potent element of the successful foreign trade is a powerful navy, not for purposes of war, but for purposes of trade. England's annual budget is more than repaid by the vastly increased trade given her by the influence of her navy. A great manufacturer of mill machinery informed me that his agent had tried for months to close a large bill in a South American city. In despair he had about given up further attempt when the accidental coming into port of one of our finest war-ships closed the contract in three days. The great Eastern and Southern trade is most peculiarly affected by exhibitions of power and permanence. As the honorable John Barrett says, before Manila it was expected that an American merchant to sell a bill of goods must keep his hat in his hand when dealing with the people who were affected by the importance of Great Britain and France as evidenced by exhibitions of naval power.

The South wishes a navy sufficiently powerful to insure this country respect on every sea and in every

9

clime. We want a navy so strong that when an American citizen sells goods in a foreign land where the laws of trade are loose, as they are in many Eastern countries, that the moral effect of a good navy will see that they are paid for value for value. We want a navy which will make the world understand that wherever an American citizen may be, in whatever country he may be trading, that this country is sufficiently powerful to protect him in all his rights and privileges. The South wants a navy sufficiently strong to let the world know that by no harsh or unfair interpretation of any country's laws, can the rights and liberties of an American citizen be violated with impunity. Ah, sir, we ask for the spirit of the old navy. Do you remember in 1853 the action of Captain Ingraham of the United States war-ship *St. Louis* in the foreign port of Smyrna? It makes the heart of an American citizen thrill when he reads the narrative. Martin Koszta, an American citizen, was imprisoned by the Austrian authorities and taken on board an Austrian ship of war which lay, with its consort, within a short distance of the *St. Louis*. The Austrian force was more than twice that of the American. To Captain Ingraham's request that Koszta be released no reply was made. A second request was made for his release by the American captain. Again it was ignored. Then rising to the measure of his great responsibility, manning a ship's boat, he sent a message to the Austrian commander that if Martin Koszta was not on board the American ship within one hour he would open fire. A half-hour passed. The anchor was weighed; the ship was put in trim for action. "Clear the quarter deck," came ringing from the American ship. Fifteen minutes only remained. "Load the guns and open the ports," was the next order. Ten minutes more ran their precious course. "Man the guns," came next. The black guns, double shotted, were run out. Complete preparation was made, the quarter deck was cleared, and every man, ready for the defence of his countryman, waited command. Captain Ingraham, with watch in hand, stood on the deck, the impersonification of the genius of Americanism. When the hands of the watch pointed to five minutes of the hour a boat was seen to put out from the Austrian ship, and within a minute of the time when with shot and shell the rights of American citizenship would have been protected, Martin Koszta, an American citizen, free and unharmed, stepped on the deck of the American man-of-war. That is the spirit of the navy we want. We desire the world to understand that we possess the ability to see the fullest protection accorded to American citizens and American interests. I wish to say, Mr. Chairman, that as an illustration of the South's devotion to American commercial interests that the new navy was largely constructed under bills introduced and pushed by a Southern man; that the largest number of vessels were added under the secretaryship of a Southern man, and that the laying of the keel of the cruiser named in honor of your beautiful city was by the direct work of a Southern man, then the chairman of the Naval Committee, and that the money which is needed by Congress to rebuild our great navy will be appropriated by the solid vote of a solid South. The South wants the navy yet stronger and will continue her policy to that end.

The Canal, with our commerce flowing through it, must be protected from the Gulf of Mexico and the Caribbean Sea just as jealously as England guards the Suez Canal from Aden, from Malta, and from Gibraltar; and the opportunities for this generation are such as will never again come without the tears and blood of the nation being poured out like rain. This is vital to our commerce. Above the cry of the demagogue striving for place, higher than the behest of party seeking advantage, there is a great and solemn view to be taken by this people, and that is the protection of our commerce in the very heart of our civilization.

The control of the Gulf of Mexico and the Caribbean Sea is essential to our commerce. Without these seas under our control, we will have built a beautiful house and left the door wide open with the rich jewels in full view of those who wish to take them. In this demand the South for one hundred years has urgently persisted. Says Napoleon, as colossal in his mastery of trade as of war, "Whatever nation holds the Mississippi and the Gulf of Mexico would be the most powerful on earth." It is looking forward; but, as a great writer

has well said, this generation is but a trustee for the
next, and when the nations of the earth are moving up
their pickets and advancing the vanguard of commerce,
trade, and power, this nation is the trustee of the generation succeeding at an awful moment. When once
the canal is built, the outposts of European commerce
will have advanced to our very doors, and whilst the
great commercial power of the world is to-day our
friend, the portentous warning of the Father of his
country as to the instability of the friendship of nations
should be heeded.

Here, at the mouth of the Mississippi, is garnered
the wealth of the Great Valley, and through the Gulf
of Mexico and the Caribbean Sea every vessel, ladened
with the products of your manufactories, must take its
way to the East and the South. Here your cottons,
your woollens, your iron products, your thousand products of loom and manufactory of the North will meet
the rare woods, rich spices, indigo, quinine, the India-
rubber, the coffee, the sugar, and the cocoa of the rich
valley of South America and the varied products from
the Far East. In these two seas, the Mediterranean
of America, meet and commingle the mighty floods
of the Amazon and the Mississippi with their products
so essential to our civilization. We should absolutely
dominate these seas. Here will be the centre of the
greatest maritime trade in the world. The islands of
these seas will be supreme over the richest territory in
the world, the heart and centre of the United States,

the great valley of the Mississippi. Interference with its trade means ruin to the trade in Newark as well as to New Orleans. Every entrance and every passage of these seas are controlled by the islands of Hayti and Jamaica. From the security of her great harbor England can easily destroy your trade through the Canal. Thirty years hence, with our hundred millions of people, the arresting of our commerce for a month will mean hunger and want. Should not the nation contemplate at an early day the purchase and control of the island of Jamaica, and the control of the island of Hayti? To-day, I boldly say it, every reason of humanity, of business, or political statesmanship, demands our control of the island of Hayti. Once the richest of France's possessions, teeming with natural advantages only given to few lands, with fertile soil, rich forests, precious minerals, and a glorious climate, situated strategically so that it can easily control the entrance of the Caribbean Sea, lying between the island of Cuba and our island of Puerto Rico, it should be a paradise.

Notwithstanding these surpassing advantages, with the very air surrounding it filled with the genius of our civilization, humanity weeps when it contemplates the barbarous horrors enacted daily within this beautiful island. Voodooism, with its nameless horror and shame; cannibalism, so open that the offenders are not tried; religion, almost a mockery; free government, a laughable travesty were it not for its bloody horrors; murder of the citizens without trial or jury; bloody

revolutions as frequent as the rains; the brutal Soulou-
que, the horrible Hippolyte, the crafty and fierce
Heureaux, bloody, red-handed tyrants masquerading
under the form of free government, compose the shock-
ing scenes of the horrid panorama. I repeat that the
horrors of suffering Cuba are more than equalled in
their intensity and terror by the bloody dramas which,
for the last fifty years, have been and are being enacted
in the island of Hayti.

Then, sir, I suggest that the highest exercise of
humanity, buttressed by a statesmanship looking to
the control of the natural seat of the world's commerce, demands our absolute dominance of the Gulf
of Mexico and the Caribbean Sea. To absolutely control these islands should be our policy. To protect our
rich Southern seacoasts and harbors and to hold in
our hands these great seas and their islands is and has
ever been the policy of the Southern statesman, and
notably that of Mr. Jefferson.

In a necessarily hurried manner, Mr. Chairman, I
have attempted merely to call attention to the great
questions which are to-day confronting the American
commercial interests, and which affect the life of this
great Republic, as it has now reached the period in its
life when its busy people cannot consume that which
is manufactured in its workshops. It is a critical
period, and the question for us to consider is whether
we will grasp the great markets within our hand and
thus have plenty and prosperity, or whether we will

continue at home and contest among ourselves for the manufacture and sale of that which we alone consume.

What will be the effect of the consummation of these great policies upon the country when, through the steady influence and help of the South, they have been carried to their full and complete fruition? My plain words cannot paint the glory of our marvellous civilization. The East and the West will then have joined their hands and the sweet mercies of the reign of Him who loves all men will, through our civilization, be offered to those who are to-day in darkness. For commerce is the greatest of missionaries and trade the greatest civilizer. Our own beautiful country will know no North and no South, no East nor no West, but all will be joined together by the eternal bonds of a busy and prosperous commercial life which has bound together beyond the question of division every section of this mighty Union. The seas of the world will be white with our sails and the laugh of the American sailor will be heard in every port known to trade. The blessings of your commerce will touch alike the dwellers under the snows of the North and under the warm sun of the Tropics. Prosperity will reign here in our land and millions of our citizens, prosperous, happy, and contented, will be sending the products of their tireless energies to other lands and other seas.

The broad avenues of your beautiful city, bordered with the ladened warehouses crowded with the rich stuffs and precious wares and strange peoples, will stretch their imperial length to your broad bay. Your river widened and the bay deepened by our Southern help and vote will bear on their proud bosoms the fleets of the Orient and Occident. The rich spices, the precious woods, and the fruits of South America will here find their best market. The curious wares and useful products of Asia, Africa, and the Islands of the Sea will crowd your wharves, and the white cotton, the corn, and the oil from my own rich South will pay their honest tribute to the glory of your city. The crown of the city will be the commerce of all the nations. Peoples from the far lands of the world will crowd your splendid colleges and schools to learn from you the teachings of our marvellous civilization. Instead of your thousand manufactories, the now silent flats will glow with forge and shop. Where the loon sounds its lonesome call and the gull wings his lazy flight, will be heard the shuttle as it flies and the click and rattle of shop and the roar of crowded railroad. Here will be witnessed the true greatness of a free people, not measured by battles or war, but by a constitution-loving people carrying its liberal laws, its intelligence, its energy, to the dark places of the world and reverently giving to a constitution, untouched by imperialism or kingship, unbroken in letter or spirit, the tribute of a people who, under God, ascribe to that glorious covenant of their liberties all the blessings which have crowned their work.

When in my vision I see the greatness of the city,

the Orchard of the Pines rises to my view, the sweet
lake and the soft sun, with Ben Hur and Sheik Ilderem
gently pressing each other with gifts. "Think what
thou hast done for me. All the spears now masterless
will come to me, and my sword hands multiply past
counting. Thou dost not know what it is to have
sway of the Desert such as will now be mine. I tell
thee it will bring tribute incalculable from commerce,
and immunity from kings. Ay, by the sword of Solomon! doth my messenger seek favor for me with Cæsar,
that will he get."

We ask in return for our devotion to your interests,
for our steady influence in favor of a liberal policy, a
more liberal treatment of the South. We do not ask
to advance beyond you, but hand in hand with you.
Ungrudgingly we have voted to deepen your harbors
and widen your rivers until now the world's commerce
can ride in safety in your harbors and at your wharves.
The South now needs your help. Your commercial
supremacy is as closely bound up in deepening our
rivers and harbors as is that of the South. You are
leading the vanguard for the capture of the trade of the
world. To succeed against the nations you must have
your raw material for manufacture at the lowest cost.
The granary of Africa was not more necessary to Rome
than the cotton, the coal, the coke, the iron, the lumber,
and the oil of the South are to you. This must come to
you by the lowest rate of transportation. The difference of cost of one-half cent. per pound on your cotton

and twenty-five cents per ton on your fuel means your being undersold in the foreign market by Great Britain and Germany. A small increase in the price of fuel lays your goods down in China and Japan at a competitive loss. The deepening of our Southern harbors and rivers that our products may reach your furnaces and mills at a minimum price means your underselling the world. With our harbors deepened and our rivers unlocked, you have, at a minimum, that which will place you beyond competition. It means more than cheap raw material to you. In a night the South has grown into a great manufacturing region. Only last month, accompanied by General Meany, a distinguished citizen of your city, intimately familiar with the South, who, notwithstanding the cares of a great business, is an able and comprehensive student of these great changing commercial conditions, I stood in a Southern city and watched the building of a great factory where five millions of dollars were being rapidly turned into two hundred thousand cotton spindles. Before this year shall have run its course, five millions of cotton spindles will be singing their merry music in the South. A Southern state to-day sets the price of pig-iron throughout the world. South Carolina is second to Massachusetts in the manufacture of cotton. Our whole attention is now devoted to manufacturing our natural products. We are just learning where lies their real value. We were poor, our cities were quiet, our pockets were empty, our fields were worn out, until we learned from you the marvellous lessons of manufacturing. It is making us rich and powerful, and year by year we will reserve an increased proportion of our natural product for our own manufacture. These conditions will be more intense in the future than in the past. For only in the last few years has the product of the manufactory exceeded the capacity of this country to consume. It must be the policy of the North to give our various manufactured products the greatest opportunity, through our own deep harbors, to reach the people of the world, rather than to cast this great trade inland to become a competitor of your mills. We do not wish this condition to arise. Instead of being your competitor in business, we wish, through our own ports, to go out into the world as your brother and helper. You will observe, gentlemen, that in nearness to raw material, cheapness of labor, and in general trade conditions, manufacturing is done far more cheaply in the South than elsewhere. To-day, that which is your commercial interest is as surely ours.

Sir, more than this do we ask. We ask a broader Americanism on your part and a better understanding and appreciation of the great section which I so unworthily represent. In all tenderness and love we ask that you will not take the statement of the scheming demagogue with his flame of fire, nor that of the partisan newspaper whose highest ambition is to obey the dictates of Party. The South comes to-day with clean hands and asks your own judgment, your own investi-

gation. We trust you implicitly. The honest, substantial sentiment of the North is what we crave.
With the great growth of the South we are part and
parcel of your life, industrial and social. No two
sections of the Union have their lives so intertwined.
Without the essentials of the South your great trade
would wither. From the great Empire of the South
you can draw every primary element of industrial life
—your cotton, your lumber, your cheapest and best
coal and coke and iron. In the future, far more than
in the past, will you be dependent upon our great
natural products to keep your forges blazing and your
manufactories at their ceaseless work. From our mines
you draw your largest dividends and from our forests
daily comes to you a king's ransom. The railroads
you have built in the South are the finest revenue pro-
ducers in the world ; and from your cotton mills, which
you have reared in the South, your dividends are thrice
greater than from your mills in the North. From the
boundless wealth of our Southern land we can give
you, in rich profusion, all of the elements needed by
you in your foreign trade. Our importance in your
world of industry is too permanent, too important for
your estimate of us to be taken second-hand. Then,
when our lives are so intertwined, he who interferes
with our relations and thorough understanding is
treading on ground consecrated to the welfare of this
great Republic.

We wish you to become more thoroughly acquainted

with our great section.   No country can become really great unless it is acquainted with the resources of each part.   We wish you to know of our mountains of iron and coal.   We want you to see the wealth of our unbroken forests, sufficient to supply the world.   We wish to show you the teeming wealth of our soil and our multitudinous natural advantages.   And above all, we wish you to understand and appreciate the kindliness and liberality of the Southern people and of our ability and desire to carefully protect the property of those who have invested their capital with us.   We are not without sin.   The great conflict left us with fortunes destroyed and hampered by another race equal to us under the law, but unequal to us in its traditions and civilization.   With no precedents in civilization to guide us, we have made mistakes; but we ask that you will try to understand our position and let nothing interfere with that better knowledge of a people so close and necessary to your greatness.

Under conditions which rarely ever before confronted a people, we have taken up the rebuilding of the State, the rehabilitating and glorifying of the South.   We twine our arms around her because we have been through sorrows with her, and you know the tender sympathy between those who have together mingled their tears.   But, sir, there have been no idle tears; there has been no dreaming in these years since the war.   We have not waited for the coming of the white sails of the ships from over the summer seas.   As

Dr. J. William Jones, the old Chaplain of the Army of Northern Virginia, my boyhood friend, was passing along the road after the war, he saw a young man ploughing in the field, guiding the plough with one hand, while an empty sleeve hung at his side. When nearer, he recognized the ploughman as a young man whom he had known in the army, who had been reared in the greatest affluence, and had been accustomed to every luxury. Being deeply touched when he saw his young friend, maimed in body and destroyed in fortune, at work, with the walls of the broken house and the fenceless field, sad reminders of what had been a happy home, he called to him and expressed the tenderest sympathy for his saddened condition in life. Straightening himself up, with a happy smile, the young man answered: "Oh, Brother Jones, that is all right. I thank God that I have one arm left and an opportunity to use it for those I love." With this inspiration twining itself around our lives, permeating and strengthening us for our struggle, the field has put on its green, the old house has been recovered, the fences have been rebuilt, and the South, your co-worker in an industrial empire, is walking proudly by your side. Hallowed by such associations, the click of the reaper as it cuts the yellow grain, the whir of the cotton spindles and the rattle of the manufactory as they float over the Southern fields, are to me the sweetest music ever heard by mortal ears.

We are brothers in this Republic of Trade. **We are**

co-heirs in the greatest civilization which the world has
ever seen.   We are the same in blood, in race, and in
traditions.   Together we have blazed out the broadest
path in the world's civilization.   Together we have
builded a government more glorious than any ever
touched by human hands or inspired by human thought.
Together we have stood in the ranks in the defence of
its eternal principles.   Then, sir, as a people united
not alone by the bonds of mere governmental measures,
but by the better and dearer ties of a people necessary
to each other, appreciating, understanding, and minis-
tering to each other.

> " In the room
> Of this grief-shadowed present, there shall be
> A Present in whose reign no grief shall gnaw
> The heart, and never shall a tender tie
> Be broken ! in whose reign the eternal Change
> That waits on growth and action shall proceed
> With everlasting Concord hand in hand."

But yesterday the sweet voice of Henry Grady was
hushed, and every patriot mourned the loss of him who
was binding together the broken bonds and healing
the wounds yet not closed.   In the city of Buffalo last
month the one upon whom his mantle has fallen and
whose lips are attuned to the sweetness of that great
follower of Him who said, " Love your enemies and
bless them that curse you," teaching the sweetness of
love, of faith, and of hope, in touching and tender

words pictured the faith of the toiler in the fields as the sweet bells of the Angelus came through the glory of the autumn sunset summoning his soul to prayer ere the evening of the day.   Many of us have been touched and helped by the holy significance of the spirit of the simple faith breathed by the Angelus and so beautifully interpreted by the great orator.   When reading his sweet words where he so aptly taught the faith and hope of the lowly workman, there arose to my mind a picture teaching to me a far holier and sweeter lesson than that of the bowed toiler of the Angelus.   It hangs in a little cottage home in the Blue Ridge of Virginia under the fragrant shade of the whispering pines, where the mountain and the valley gently touch and kiss each other into kindness. The simple picture has none of the surroundings of the Angelus, no mellowed, artful light, no golden frame, no thrill of reverent obeisance for the dead painter who so wonderfully interpreted for mankind the sweet spirit of Faith and Hope.   Its frame is formed of the brown birchen bark, and decorated with the cone of the mountain pine.   It was not created by the cunning hand of a great painter, but it is a simple wood-cut, representing a broken mountain plain in the gray morning of an April day.   In the misty foreground there stands an army of men, with want and sorrow pinching and distressing them, with their ragged gray uniforms hanging in tatters from their gaunt forms, with bowed heads and swimming eyes, with ruin and disaster surrounding them like grim phantoms. Over beyond them is a gray-eyed man with his slouch hat in his hand. It is Grant at Appomattox, and he is saying to Lee's broken army, there will be no Roman triumphs, no passing under the yoke, no humiliation, no imprisoning. "Men, go home and take your horses with you. You will need them to put in your crops." Great commander! splendid leader! friend of the South! whose memory will ever sit enshrined in the hearts of the sons of Lee's ragged soldiers at Appomattox. Before the picture of this exceeding charity the notes of the Angelus grow soft,

> " Your voices break and falter in the darkness,
>   Break, falter, and are still,"

and touch but gently the souls of those, who, bowing their heads, wait for the inspiration which comes from their mellow cadence. The Angelus teaches Faith and Hope, but the little woodcut, resting under the benison of the Blue Virginia mountains, voices a Charity beyond compare. "And now abideth faith, hope, and charity, these three, but the greatest of these is charity." Gathering the spirit of the great commander and holding the glory of his exceeding charity before us as an inspiration and guide, let us consecrate ourselves to the immolation of the wounds and sorrows and uncharities of the sad old past on the glowing and rekindled altars of a re-united Nation. For, oh, my brothers, there is something that we of the South desire that is more boundless than your commerce, richer by far than your gold and silver and your gems, more yearned for by us than your broad harbors filled with the ladened ships of the nations, and more priceless to us than the fruit of your looms and your shops and your manufactories. Something before which gross utilitarianism and materialism are but ashes and dust. We want your love. Ours in all of its plenitude and richness we freely give to you, and withhold of it not a jot or a tittle. The winds to-night, whispering over the mountains of my far-away Southern home, softly sing of our boundless charity and love. The sweet Southern sun has long ago kissed away the crimson stains from our fields, and our hearts are as redolent of charity and love as the magnolia and the lily are of their sweetness and perfume. The nodding cotton ball and the meadows richly green are fast covering the rent and hurt of war. The great heart of the South is full and yearns for its once estranged brother with a love that passeth all understanding. Our old battle flags are laid away in that hallowed ark of the household where lie the faded glove, the old lace collar, the worn garments, the little keepsakes, the lock of hair of our mothers, and the little worn child's shoe with sweet enchantment bringing to memory's silent halls the lullaby of little feet, and on those sacred days when with reverent hands we tenderly touch them and gently smooth away the wrinkles of time, the faint odor of rosemary and lavender breathes only of love and ten-

derness. With outstretched hands, we of the South
ask your love, your charity, and tenderness, and within
the touch of the most memorial year when we on the
battle-fields of the nation have commingled the consecrated blood of the North and the South, upon whom-
soever for partisan purposes, or private or political gain,
would rekindle the fires of sectional hate, we would
invoke the thunders of Him who holds the nations in
the hollow of His hand. Then, my brothers, with
your strong arms about the South, strengthened, en-
couraged, united, and glorified, the world would hear
the majestic and solemn tread of a free and constitution-
loving people carrying its civilization and commerce
and its religion to the nations of the uttermost parts of
the earth. Without irreverence, with this great glory
trembling upon us, in the words of the old Prophet of
the Most High, " Behold thou shalt call a nation that
thou knowest not, and a nation that knew not thee
shall run unto thee, because of the Lord thy God, and
for the Holy One of Israel, for he hath glorified thee."

IV
THE ELECTIVE FRANCHISE

D E TOCQUEVILLE, the aristocratic delineator of American Democracy, narrates that in his travels into the primeval America he arrived upon the shores of a crystal lake, embosomed in untouched forests; that in the midst of the lake was a beautiful islet, shaded to the banks with trees old as the daylight of time. He crossed over to the island and was delighted with the richness of the soil and the exuberance of growth of tree and flower, and was awed by the silence and beauty and solitude of the scene. However, amidst the majesty of this morning of nature, he found upon the island some remains of man. Upon careful inspection he discovered, amidst the glory of nature, where a European had made his home. But how changed! The logs of the cabin had fallen to the ground and had sprouted anew, and over their remains had grown the flower and the tree. The scattered stones of the hearth lay under the fallen chimney and were blackened with the old fire, and were over-scattered with the thin ashes of another day. He stood in silent admiration of the glories of nature and the littleness of man, and as he left the solitude he exclaimed with melancholy, "Are the ruins, then, already here?"

So, Mr. President, when I received from your able and courteous secretary the formulation of the question for discussion, which betokens within itself that, whilst we are in the very glory of the dawn of our day, the sacred temple of our hopes and love was broken, I was led to exclaim with the old philosopher, "Are the ruins, then, already here?"

In my poor way, I will this evening examine the sacred edifice, and we will together touch its walls and attempt to ascertain whether foundation and lintel and jam and turret stand true and plumb as when they left the hands of the master builders; for, as Mr. Lowell relates, when Guizot once asked " How long I thought the Republic would last?" " I replied," said he, " so long as the ideas of the men who founded it continue dominant." Do we not all assent to his reply?

The formulation of the subject for investigation, " Does the experience of this Republic up to the close of the nineteenth century justify universal manhood suffrage, or should the elective franchise be limited by education, property, or other qualification," carries in it the most important and vital questions of our civil life.

The question is of to-day, and I will not take precious time to present the rubbish of the history of the franchise. A word, however, is necessary that we may intelligently grasp the conditions of the early days of the Republic and understand their influence upon the present. Being a Virginian, I will be excused by the indulgent audience for having taken Virginia as a general type showing the evolution of the present franchise condition.

The status in Virginia explains why the Fathers, when they annunciated the great salient principles of free government, a radical departure in the lines of government, did not also announce manhood suffrage, the present essence of democracy.

Necessarily, when the great truths of representative government were proclaimed by the Fathers, they could not at once disembarrass themselves from all of the accompaniments of government as theretofore experienced by them. It is generally understood that the limitation of suffrage to freeholders, which practically made an aristocratic government, and the equal representation of the counties, which was sectional, were voluntarily adopted by the people of Virginia. Such was not the case. This limitation of suffrage to freeholders was the result of the commands of the King of England, and these commands were enforced by the bayonets of two regiments of his soldiers, and it was without any act of assembly. Thus, at the time of the Revolution, for more than a century freehold government had been the practical law of the people. Yet it was contrary to the salient principles of the peoples' free government. The question then naturally arises, why was this system continued after the people had substituted their own in place of the rule of the King of England? This is frequently asked by those who look toward the reimposition of suffrage limitation.

In Virginia when the convention of 1776 met and adopted its Declaration of Rights :

That all men are by nature, equal, free, and independent ;

That all power is vested **in,** and consequently derived from, the people ;

That government is and ought to be instituted for the common benefit, protection, and security of the people ; and

That a majority of the people hath an indubitable, inalienable, and indefeasible right to act for the public weal ;

there was then in the condition of affairs a practical necessity for the continuation of the anomaly of freehold suffrage. The convention, composed of some of the greatest and wisest of the Fathers of the Republic, was sitting within sight of the bayonets of the King of Great Britain, and within sound of his cannon. They had inaugurated the war in which every right of life and property was imperilled. The freeholders were a great and powerful body upon whom was the chief reliance for defence against the tyranny of England, and hence they adopted the proposition that the right of suffrage "shall remain as at present exercised." There was no time to change and pull down and build up. It was the time to fight. The Fathers thoroughly understood the controvention of the principles announced by them and as set out by their theory of government. Mr. Jefferson earnestly insisted that the people, "So soon as leisure should be afforded them for entrenching within good form the rights for which they had bled," should do so. This demand for equal exercise of suffrage never afterwards was at rest. Alike in the North as in Virginia the demand was unceasing on the part of the plain people that they should have a part in the management as they had in the perils of the government. This culminated in Virginia in the memorial of 1829 presented to the convention by John Marshall, in which the following pregnant words occur :

"If we are sincerely republican, we must give our confidence to the principles we profess. We have been taught by our fathers that all power is vested in, and derived from, the people ; not the freeholders ; that the majority of the community, in whom abides the physical force, have also the political right of creating and remoulding at will, their civil institutions. Nor can this right be anywhere more safely deposited. The generality of mankind, doubtless, desire to become owners of property ; left free to reap the fruits of their labors, they will seek to acquire it honestly. It can never be their interest to overburden, or render precarious, what they themselves desire to enjoy in peace. But should they ever prove as base as the argument supposes, force alone, arms, not votes, could effect their designs ; and when that shall be attempted, what virtue is there in Constitutional restrictions, in mere wax and paper, to withstand it? To deny to the great body of the people all share in the government, on suspicion that they may deprive others of their property; to rob them in advance of their rights; to look to a privileged order as the fountain and depositary of all power is to depart from the fundamental maxims, to destroy the chief beauty, the characteristic feature, indeed, of Republican Government.''

In 1849, these words became true in Virginia as well in practice as in theory.

And generally throughout the Republic at this period there rested the strife between the mighty spirits of Alexander Hamilton and Thomas Jefferson, the one living in latter days in the stately steppings of Daniel Webster, and the other, passing strange for a Virginian to say, reincarnated in the tall form and furrowed brow and catholic spirit of Abraham Lincoln.

What has been the effect of universal suffrage upon the great living principles of our government? Whither has been the trend, upward or downward? Has it strengthened or pauperized the fundamental principles which we have been taught were the abiding glory of free government? How has it affected the relation of the citizen to the local government, to the town, to the city, to the State, and to the Union; the relation between the State and the National Government; and the relation between the classes composing this free government? These questions, while allowing no touch of poetry or opportunity for the play of fancy, are vital, and their general principles alone can be here considered.

How has universal suffrage affected the principle of local self-government, for as one of the great living heads of my profession, Judge Dillon, well says, " and local self-government, it cannot be too often enforced, is the true and only solid basis of our free institutions "?

This is the first relation of the citizen to government, and it is the fundamental idea of our governmental life because it affects the immediate daily life of the citizen. This primary exercise of the rights of citizenship is so important that I will be pardoned for a little elementary discussion, for a free people should never become tired of contemplating the first steps of free institutions.

The borough-mote in Old England preserved and cultured the vital spark of Teutonic liberty. The borough bell was the living resonant signal as far as its piercing clang could reach, warning fierce baron and greedy churchman and grasping king that the Englishman held to his local rights, even if these rights required his blood.

This is the principle which has distinguished Old England from the other nations of the world, her resolute clinging to the primal principles of her government. In the borough alone was the right of free speech in open meeting. Here alone in all of the Kingdom was the right of self-government, and above all, here was the right of trial by one's peers. " Had Kebel been a dweller within the borough," said the Burgesses, " he would have gotten his acquittal as our liberty is." Under Angevin and Saxon the local power of self-government was resolutely defended. Sometimes it was paid for in money, more often in blood ; but at whatever price, it was gotten, despite conflict, bloody though it may have been, or price however high. Then as now the borough was the schoolhouse of liberty. Here were discussed, and often-times fiercely discussed, the first beginnings and principles of free government; for the settlement of these principles affected the immediate welfare of the community, and frequently the personal liberty of its inhabitants. " Let the City of London have all its old liberties and its free customs as well by land as water, besides this I will and grant, that all other cities, boroughs, and towns and ports have all of their liberties and free customs," rang the clarion note of the Great Charter. " They have given me four and twenty over kings," exclaimed John Lackland, as he gnashed his teeth in his anguish, but as usual he was mistaken in the people, for instead of twenty-four over kings, he had placed for all time the written guarantees of local government, the very germ of liberty, in the hands of all of his people.

More than five hundred years afterwards, in a new country, the American Revolution broke out, says De Tocqueville, and the doctrine of the sovereignty of the people grew out of the township and took possession of the State.

For taking away our charters, abolishing our most valuable laws, suspending our own Legislatures, ran the indignant protest of the Declaration of Independence.

Here, then, for the first time, voluntarily, in the history of government, was there incorporated in the initiative life of a State, the full, free, and unqualified consent of the law-making power to the principle of local self-government. We have changed the borough and the town to the magisterial and school district, the town, the village, and the city, but have only transferred to our citizens the doctrine as well as the traditions of the grandest figure in the history of free government, the English borough-man. Sir, it seems to me that if I could make the stricken marble glow with living life, it would not speak in the image of stern Puritan or belted Virginian Cavalier, as typical of our political being, great though their lessons have been ; but rather would I create as the chiefest figure of our civil life the English borough-man, holding in his strong and resolute hands, against all comers, the right of free speech, of free local government, and the right of trial by jury.

How, then, under the exercise of universal suffrage do we stand to-day in the evolution of local political government ? The insistent demand of the citizen, following the English tradition, is for the free control of local matters, concerning the local interests of township, district, or county, as the years roll on, the demand is becoming more potent within their respective limitations that the local government must be uninterfered with and uncontrolled. Local self-government was never so potent in the history of civil government as it is to-day. In education, police, and fiscal affairs its principles have manifestly broadened and strengthened since the advent of universal suffrage. In every State, we see the citizen strengthening his local government by careful legislative enactment controlling the management of his local business. Universal suffrage has peculiarly intensified the desire for, and benefit of, local self-government, for the obvious reason that the local government deals not with the few great questions, but rather with the every-day small affairs of life in which the every-day small people, unlearned and learned, whether owning property or not, are directly interested. This growth of the desire for local self-government is well illustrated by the increasing legislation in all of the States, providing for the election of district and township officers rather than their appointment by a central body such as the County Court. This principle has vindicated the great and persistent contention of our English ancestry by its history in our Union, for local self-government, under universal suffrage, has increased its efficiency in promoting public good by decreasing taxation, increasing the educational facilities, and taking direct charge of and improving the police and fiscal affairs. Here do we behold the action of the people directly upon public affairs, untrammelled by political thought and uninterfered with by the demand of party loyalty. Then, Sir, we believe that in this important feature we see one of the peculiar triumphs of our present franchise system, for in every State, on the prairie and in the mountain, in agricultural as well as in commercial and manufacturing communities, we behold the extending, by careful enactment under universal suffrage, of the local self-governing institutions, which called from Thomas Jefferson the expression, "Those wards, called townships in England, are the vital principles of their governments, and have proved themselves the wisest invention ever devised by the wit of man for the perfect exercise of self-government and for the preservation of liberty."

Let us briefly consider the citizen in his relation to a larger and wider sweep of local self-government than that of the borough, county, or town. The American city has given to universal suffrage its severest trial. Here has certainly been presented the hardest conditions attending any exercise of universal suffrage. Let us for a moment discuss the conditions presented to the franchise by the American city. They are unique in the whole history of civil government. In the first place, those who exercise the franchise in most great cities are largely foreign, either by birth or immediate lineage. They have had no experience whatever in the art of government, and in most instances they belonged to the governed class. The American city is growing wondrously in wealth, size, and power, and its streets, parks, schools, hospitals, and all public institutions and their administration are not the results of centuries of civic evolution, as is the case in Europe.   They are urgently demanded, at once, and on a colossal scale, and must be administered with no guiding precedent. They are created practically out of the ground.   They can not, as in Europe, be added to here, or patched there, and the fault of this century corrected in the next.   Their evolution from town to city can not run along with the evolution of the people from barbarism to civilization, and thus have relations which gradually adjust themselves to abiding and final conditions. They must spring into life full panoplied for the needs of a vastly growing and exacting population.

"It is not strange that the people educating and ex- perimenting on city government, for which there is absolutely no precedent, under conditions of exceptional difficulty, should have to stumble toward correct and successful methods through experience, which may be both costly and distressing," says a great authority. Thus the city has a burden of educating the governing population whose idea of government is entirely low, and, concurrently, the city must take care of its material growth and carry on all of the practical details of gov- ernment.   This growth in its haste has produced extra cost in the creation and exercise of municipal institu- tions, and has naturally afforded unexampled oppor- tunity for municipal crime.   Notwithstanding these conditions, the spirit of our free institutions has created in the American city a marvel of efficient local government, and has raised it, in practically one lifetime, to the height of commercial glory and to unapproachable civil magnificence. "Looked at in this light," says the same authority, "the moral would seem to be, not so much that the American cities are justly criticizable, but that results so great have been achieved in so short a time."

Considering this unique condition of municipal population and growth, the cities of this country, as a rule, under the influence of universal suffrage, are well governed. It is true, in many instances, we have the Boss, and the Ring Rule, and, as compared with the result, small deficiencies in effective government. But should we not consider the ultimate result of our system of general suffrage in the city? Broadway may not be always well swept, but our franchise system embracing all the people has made it the greatest street in the world. This great city, oftentimes, may have ineffective management of its politics and finances, but its great harbor is crowded with the ships of all the nations, and the world bows to its unapproachable civil grandeur. Again, it has been frequently made the illustration of bad civil government under the rule of the people endowed with the universal franchise, but has not this universal franchise created the greatest city on this continent? We hear of much vice in the city, but I challenge a comparison of New York City with London or Paris. Do we sufficiently consider ultimate results when we are discussing the political management of civil government, both city and state? Beyond question, there has been municipal crime, but whenever it has been ascertained public sentiment has demanded, and in most instances effected, the punishment of the criminal. When we speak of municipal crime, does it compare, in anywise, with the scandals and the crime arising from the opening and improving of the new Paris? Is it to be mentioned with the municipal crimes of London twenty years ago after its thousand years of existence? Are not the results of popular control to be commended somewhat when you have the best system of public schools, of charity and correction, of fire protection, of parks and streets in the known world?

It is true that the ideal of government of a portion of the population of the city is low, but would it not be fraught with infinite evil to keep it at that level by withholding the franchise from a large part of the population? Without argument, what effect upon the city would the vast foreign born element of this city have if debarred from the great social and educational benefit derived from the exercise of the franchise? Which is worse in a free government, a badly swept street, or thousands of discontented people walking the clean one? Surely, in a popular government, what cause of discontent could be so potent as the debarring from the franchise? As a general rule, there have been crime and mismanagement in the American cities, yet under the exercise of the universal franchise the American city has steadily grown and is growing better. The elections are fairer, the schools infinitely better, the streets are cleaner, the finances more honestly administered than they were ten years ago, and I appeal to your own experience to know if every general condition of municipal government is not improving under the practical application of the present system of suffrage. The cities of smaller size are practically well governed, and in almost every State in the Union the laws governing the cities and the application of them are vastly improved. Every year witnesses the increase in the number of States, which provide in their constitutions against special charters being made for cities, and a number of States are conferring upon the cities the right to approve their charters before they go into operation.

Says President Seth Low, at whose feet as at those of a master do I sit when studying this interesting question of municipal government, "Every one understands that universal suffrage has its drawbacks, and in cities these defects become especially evident. It would be uncandid to deny that many of the problems of American cities spring from this factor. Especially because the voting population is continually swollen by foreign emigrants whom time alone can educate into an intelligent harmony with the American system. But because there is a scum upon the surface of a boiling liquid it does not follow that the material nor the process to which it is subjected is itself bad. Universal suffrage as it exists in the United States is not only a great element of safety in the present day and generation, but is perhaps the mightiest educational force to which the masses of men have been exposed. . . . It is probable that no other system of government would have been able to cope any more successfully on the whole with the actual condition that American cities have been compelled to face."

Pursuing this "Hierarchy of Liberty," let us briefly consider the next higher relation of the citizen to government. Has a half century of universal suffrage preserved the institutional rights of the State? This is most important in determining whether a modification should be made in the existing system, for during this period the spirit of Democracy speaking through universal suffrage has exercised unlimited control of the institutions of our government, and could at will change or destroy. Those who formed this government knew not well the power they were creating. They had only before them the ancient Democracies, which universally, from the impulses of passion or of interest, destroyed existing conditions and disregarded organic rights. The Fathers wished to adopt a plan of government which, while it would be democratic, yet no power of the majority could interfere and destroy certain rights and organic principles. Hence they created the judiciary, a selected few, and practically said that this department of democratic government,

within constituted limitations, should be the casting
and controlling voice as to the rights most sacred to
the people. It was certainly a bold idea in the new
system of democratic government to allow a few to
settle the great questions affecting the many. Yet to-
day, although the decisions of the courts have been
oftentimes contrary to the judgment of the people and
sometimes even oppressive, yet the spirit of democracy
dominated by the universal suffrage of the people has
left unimpaired in power and in dignity the courts of
the land. Nay more, appreciating that national and
state life can only live through the stable and impartial
spirit of justice, it has enlarged and widened the powers
of the courts until to-day, in the estimation of the people, and in fact, they embody the highest and most
sublime attributes of this free nation.

The Fathers having in mind the immense powers of
the executive head of the British Government gave the
veto power sparingly and grudgingly to the executives
of the States, yet the people under the influences of
universal suffrage have doubly guaranteed the States
against their own acts, and during the life-time of the
present system of franchise have practically given the
salutary power of veto, excepting possibly in two or
three instances, to the governor of every State in the
Union.

The fear has been on the part of those interested in
our institutions that the majority, uncontrolled, would
weaken and practically destroy the binding and organic

powers of the State constitutions, and introduce a doctrine of loose interpretation of their important provisions. What has been the result? Constitutional provisions created in the early days of the States, so far as the people are concerned, have been strengthened in detail and particular until every organic right of to-day is protected as never before in the history of civil government.

Instead of license and instability of organic government, universal suffrage has increased conservatism, and in one hundred years only the post-bellum amendments have been added to the Constitution, and unless it is absolutely and potently demanded an amendment to the State constitution universally meets defeat at the hands of the people.

Although the legislatures are the nearest representative agents of the people, still by constitutional enactment the legislatures of the States are hedged about by stringent provisions, holding them to strict accountability in every sense of their legislative life.

The great principles of Magna Charta, those primordial rights as to life, liberty, and property, under our suffrage system, have been strengthened by the people; and year by year, in essence and by legislative enactment, they have become the increasing breath of the State. Universal suffrage has accentuated the sacred rights of free speech, the freedom of religion, the supremacy of the civil over the military authority, the rights of the press, and the sacredness of vested property in its various forms, calling forth from Sir Henry Maine, certainly no friend of popular government, the encomium, that "all this beneficent prosperity reposes on the sacredness of contract and the stability of private property ; the first the implement, and the last the reward of success in the universal competition," and in a democrary generally emphasizing, "that this is a government of law, not of men."

Whilst the organic powers of the State have been strengthened by the people, yet State socialism under universal suffrage has not grown with the growth of the people. To live by taxation imposed by the State upon some other person and to exist by the exertion of others is the temptation of the body politic of a free government. A half century ago when the spirit of universal suffrage became the policy of our country, a great Englishman remarked, " In thirty years the American States will be cooking for the populace." Notwithstanding the unexampled and marvellous increase in the complexities of government and in the essentials of our civilization, to-day, whilst the people hold absolutely in their strong hands the purse strings of taxation and the whole power of the State, and whilst the conditions of life have become necessarily more severe with them, yet they have not increased the sphere of the State in lifting from their oftentimes tired shoulders one burden of life. Tempted by the fair promises of party, preyed on by the demagogue, in sight of the bursting treasuries of the State, yet the sphere of the State, as expressed by the organic institutions of to-day, comprises the care of the poor and insane, the establishment of hospitals, the education of the people, the management of the State machinery, in both the spirit, and in almost the exact words, as penned by the hands of the Constitution makers of a century ago. Whenever an enlightened socialism has enlarged this sphere of the State it has always been a necessary concomitant of, and logical sequence to, these original organic powers of the State and never for the individual material benefit of the citizen. The Patriarcha is still a dream as it was in the days of Sir Robert Filmer, and universal suffrage has not purchased the ease of the people at the price of the paternalism of the State. It has grasped the principles of universal education as the broadest and best foundation for republican institutions ; and whilst the State succeeded the Church as the controlling influence in directing education, still under pressure, oftentimes great, the people have resolutely clung to the principles of absolute divorce from sectarian religious teaching on the part of the State. Excepting under peculiar conditions in one portion of our country, the principle of universal suffrage has been widened by the State until it enfolds all of the people. The seeming anomaly of its arrested development in one section is particularly germane to this branch of discussion, as to the relation of the people to the State, and with your permission I will briefly consider the peculiar conditions of suffrage in the South.

Will you not to-night, for a short time, listen to a Southern man, as he endeavors to lay upon your broad shoulders a little of the burden which has weighed so heavily upon the shoulders of your sisters of the South, and to explain why the march of the universal franchise has been delayed in the South? No good Southern man fears to trust implicitly the chivalry of the North. Necessarily, I can occupy but a short time upon this interesting question, and will but generally consider it.

When the war ended, from Virginia to Georgia the yellow Southern sun looked down upon ruin unparalleled in the history of civilization. The cities were destroyed, and the lands were devastated. We were without clothes, or money, or food. Our fathers and brothers were sleeping in

"The voiceless graves where dead men dream."

Our industries were paralyzed, and our civilization was uprooted. There were alone left the bright sun, the fruitful soil, and a far-away hope. These would have been sufficient foundation upon which a resolute and energetic people could have again reared an abiding and glorious civilization. But, Sir, in the years gone by, on the shores of Old Virginia, there landed a ship

"Built in the eclipse and rigged with curses dark,"

and when the man of the South lifted his despairing

eyes they beheld his former slave, uneducated, untried in government, untouched with the genius of rule, unpermeated with Americanism, sitting on the broken porticos and bestriding the fallen pillars of his State. Since Alaric and Attila scourged Europe, never has wrong so wrought upon the civilization of the world as it did in the years of Negro rule in the South. I turn with sorrow from the dreadful record, and only look back upon the wretchedness of the Past in order to explain the complexity of the Present.

The debts of the Southern States were increased four hundred millions of dollars. States were pauperized, and the millions squandered went into the hands of the Negroes and their allies, and not in the channels of good government. Debauchery ran riot, and political dishonesty held a saturnalia equalled in its unspeakable horrors only in the last days of Imperial Rome. Law was disregarded, the rights of Habeas Corpus and the great fundamental principles of Anglo-Saxon government were laughed to scorn; juries were packed and courts debauched; men were not allowed to appear in court to show cause why they should not be bereft of their remaining property. The supreme courts were travesties, and were packed or elected to do the bidding of those who wished to legalize by the terms of the law some legislative crime.

What was the natural result of this terrible condition of social and State life? Men seeing the State forever ruined, their property confiscated, their very lives in

danger, business paralyzed, taxes increased an hundred-
fold, and property destroyed, did many things, dictated
by the sole spirit of self-preservation, which were not
understood by the North at the time.

Let us speak plainly and yet with charity. We are
brothers and each wants to understand the troubles of
the other. Here has been the chief trouble in this
great question. The Negro question has been made
a political cry and the mere flotsam and jetsam of
party. It is the most important question, political as
well as economical, which has ever confronted civilization at any time or in any country. It demands all of
our power, all of our love and patience and forbearance, and should be worked out by the whole people
uninfluenced by the demagogue or the wish of party.
We, of the South, ask that you simply put yourselves
in the position of your Southern brethren. I mean, Sir,
only in your kindly imagination, for with all of the
strength of my life, I pray that you and the North may
never walk the road of suffering and sorrow as has the
South. Consider the fundamental difference in your
political and social situation and that of the South.

Your sole cause of complaint as to popular government is that you have a large number of foreigners
in your population. They are of the same blood, of
the same color, largely of the same language, and filled
with the same aspirations as yourselves, and are rapidly
assimilating with you in character and in life.

With us there is an alien race, different in color, in

life, and with whom as a primordial factor of his being the Teuton has strenuously refused to assimilate in blood, in social existence, or in government.

Mr. Chairman, to emphasize this sad condition of the South, let me say that at the time the South was placed under the feet of the Negro and his white allies, not more than one-tenth of them could read and write; and as late as 1880 only three-tenths were able to read and write.

It was Mr. Lincoln's intention to bring the States back into the Union with the white man in control. This is clearly shown by his proclamation in reference to North Carolina. His plan was to bring back this State with the voters who were qualified in 1860. These voters, of course, were the white men. Later he was in favor of allowing the intelligent Negro to vote. He penetrated more profoundly than any other statesman of his era into the deep mystery of the civil life in the South, surrounded as it was by its peculiar political and social conditions. He thoroughly understood, imbued as he was with the very genius of free government, and believing in the exercise of the franchise by all of the people, that the conditions surrounding the South were peculiar and unique, and that the franchise provisions applicable to the country at large would not apply to the South. He wrote Governor Hahn of Louisiana: " Now you are about to have a convention, which, among other things, will probably define the elective franchise, I barely suggest for your private consideration, whether some of the colored people may not be let in; as, for instance, the very intelligent, and especially those who have fought gallantly in our ranks. They would probably help in some trying time to come to keep the jewel of liberty in the family of freedom."

With that marvellous intuition into the innermost workings of the people's being, Mr. Lincoln saw then, that which cost us a third of a century of heart burnings and misunderstandings and loss to learn, that the governmental problem of the North and West to be solved by a people of the same race and color, homogeneous in educational and civil traditions, was totally different in every element from that to be worked out by the South, with its Caucasian civilization intermixed with, and oftentimes dominated in numbers by, a race different in color, genius, and tradition, and just emerging from centuries of slavery. But Mr. Lincoln's death blasted the hopes of the South, and in the war between Congress and Andrew Johnson, the South fell heir to the horrors of Reconstruction.

Then arose the Kuklux trouble, and there were passed many improvident laws by the South, and then occurred on both sides those matters, which in the heated state of public feeling, were the cause of the North and South not abiding together in peace and in unity. Truly it was a situation for the South which had no hope in its dark bosom, and however decided would mean ultimate hurt to her and her institutions.

The men of the South saw the sad ruin in character and credit, the paralysis of public and private business, and that personal and political crime was open and unabashed. They did exactly that which the people of the North would have done under the same circumstances. They asserted themselves and saved the State from the ruin impending and drove the Negro from control. Yet, on the other hand, they knew that they violated the letter of the Constitution and infringed upon the fundamental theory of our government. Every intelligent Southern man knew this and regretted the situation. Mr. Chairman, was there ever such a condition presented to a free people? To have bowed to the will of the majority, we would have beheld a land

> "Its shores
> Strewn with the wreck of fleets, where mast and hull
> Drop away piecemeal; battlemented walls
> Frown idly, green with moss, and temples stand
> Unroofed, forsaken by the worshippers.
> Foundations of old cities and long streets
> Where never fall of human foot is heard
> Upon the desolate pavement."

To do otherwise was to offend against the fundamental laws governing the life of a free government.

Now, Sir, the South intends to do away with this anomalous condition. The men of the South understand the lesson their enforced condition has compelled them to teach. They intend to work out this question under the spirit and the letter of the Constitution. The reason why this absolute fairness has been delayed was the memory of the Negro rule and control in the South, and, further, that the South did not intend to place its future with all of its marvellous possibilities in the control of the forces which wrecked it during the Reconstruction period. Whilst holding the political situation in their own hands, they propose to treat the Negro fairly under the Constitution of the country. Throughout the whole of the South, there has been, and is now, a movement for constitutional conventions in the direction of pure government. These conventions are not, as some understand, to get rid of the vote of the Negro. The white man dominates politically in every Southern State. The conventions are in the direction of constitutional government and pure elections and fairness to the Negro, and are intended as a legal and honest method by which the Southern States can relieve themselves of their trouble and perplexity and do justice to the election laws of the country, and at the same time preserve control of their civilization.

I have no intent or desire to avoid a fair statement of the situation ; but I am placing it before you in all honesty and simplicity in order that you will understand that the South is attempting, with the little light before us, to work out for this country the question which tangles our feet in whatever path we would turn.

Personally, I have earnestly urged that the South

should adopt an inflexible educational or property basis, administered fairly for both white and black. I believe that this would work out the question, and the South is gradually arriving at the conclusion that it can, by constitutional methods, preserve the spirit of the Constitution and save its civilization. It desires and intends to give the negro his constitutional rights, and has only been heretofore debarred from so doing by the fear of the destruction of that which a state holds most sacred. The energy of the South is being earnestly devoted to educating the Negro in order to, as quickly as possible, make him a good and intelligent citizen. Groping in the dark, we grant that oftentimes wrong has been done to the Negro. This the South deplores, whilst not for a moment intending to assent to the truth of the thousands of the baseless charges which have been made against her in the treatment of this question. In our impoverishment, we have given one hundred million dollars to the education of the Negro, and we are to-day impartially dividing with him our every dollar, in order that we may work out for this country and for mankind the darkest riddle which has ever con-fronted and perplexed civilization. Whilst the South is doing her part, the Negro has responded by progress in education and those virtues which will ultimately make him useful instead of a menace to civilization.

The settlement of this momentous question cannot be accomplished in a day. Time must be one of the chief factors. In adjusting the political relations of the Negro and the white man, living together, with no precedent to guide, there have necessarily resulted many mistakes. But the situation will be worked out with justice to the Negro, with honor to the white man and in consonance with the spirit of the Constitution. In the progress towards constitutional government in the South, although believing firmly in universal suffrage, many of us, friends of the Negro, have advocated a franchise limitation as an immediate step from the anomaly of to-day and towards the consummation of fair government for white and black.

This seemingly anomalous position has not been brought about by a spirit of unfairness towards the Negro or by instability of our political opinion. It does not furnish any argument for the imposition of a franchise limitation throughout the country. The situation must be looked at under the plain light. The men who believe in a franchise limitation for the South are unquestioned as to their friendship for the Negro; but they know and understand the conditions in the South. These conditions are unprecedented in political history, unexampled in civilization, and absolutely unique in their relations to the other portions of the country. In the country at large universal suffrage means civil splendor, commercial and personal welfare, pure government, peace, and progress. In the South it means prostration of the State, anarchy, commercial and personal ruin, and a war of races, destructive to State and social government. Upon one principle, however, the relations of the South to the country at large are upon the same level; and that is, whatever franchise limitations may be imposed by the South to preserve her civilization should be administered with unsparing impartiality alike for white and black, and the South intends that this shall be.

It is important to consider for a moment the effect which the era of universal suffrage has had upon the relation between the States and the National Government. The early sentiment was that universal suffrage would retard the growth of the nationality of this government. In other words, having the ancient democracies in mind, not differentiating between them and our representative system of government, many feared that, under a wide franchise, popular license would trend in the direction of the increase in the powers of the States. At that period the great preponderating powers of the States led to the free entertaining of this view. In the majority of conflicts with the National Government, the States had won. They had taken advantage of every question and doubt as to the reservation of their powers under the Constitution, and had most vigorously availed themselves of these reserved rights. Thus, at this period, the States had grown relatively so powerful that it led De Tocqueville to declare that the Union was only shadow, and that ultimately its existence would be endangered by the preponderating power of the States in the social compact. The present condition of the balance in our social affairs shows the complete failure in the prognostications of that day as to the effect of universal suffrage upon the governmental relations under the social compact. In the years of universal suffrage in this country the balance of the government has been restored, and instead of popular license and national disintegration, and the increase in the already overweening powers of the States, the National Government has been relatively strengthened. The governmental condition of to-day shows the great skill of its creation, for whilst the war left the National Government with vastly increased powers, yet the causes of friction have been largely removed between the concurrent powers under the Constitution, and there is to-day a better feeling between the States and the National Government than has ever been known in the history of our country. It gives a great impetus to optimism when we observe that, notwithstanding the great war, which was practically a war of the General Government against the sovereignty of the States, the States are to-day determined to be as absolutely sovereign within their constitutional powers as ever before. The chief fear of to-day, however, is the tendency of greatly increased power in the General Government, as the danger was fifty years ago in the enlarged powers on the part of the States. This tendency is the danger of the day.

Public sentiment, appreciating the tremendous power

which the General Government exhibited in the great civil conflict, and its consequent preponderance necessarily arising from that exhibition of strength, has been earnestly aroused in the past few years in the direction of preserving intact the constitutional rights of the States. As a great scholar well observes, "This reliance (upon national authority), however, is controlled and regulated by the deep-seated consciousness of the people that the rights of the separate States are not to be superseded by the acts of the Central Government, and that the rights of towns, counties, and districts are to be protected against the arbitrary interference of legislation." In this relation is peculiarly needed that "righting sense" of the people, undiminished in power, to watch and preserve within their respective bounds those delicate relations between the State and General Government.

Let us for a moment investigate the relations of the citizens each to the other, and, practically speaking, the effect of universal suffrage upon the classes. This has been the subject of infinite discussion by the learned. Will you pardon me for an observation as to the general consideration of this important question by the scholars? They have largely affected the public sentiment among the higher classes. The want of breadth in the elucidation of this question of universal suffrage by the learned emboldens me, a plain man, to ask for a deeper and more real knowledge of the people on the part of the learned of our country. They have wrought infinite harm to the body politic by opinions betraying want of knowledge of the people themselves, the real subject of discussion. Do not the conclusions of the learned as to the great public too frequently result from investigation and experience alike limited and indiscriminate in application? Do not those in high places most frequently neglect the strenuous exercise of that *ars profunda*, that deeper penetration into the very life and genius of the people? That subtle spirit, that vital essence of the people's being, is the most difficult to grasp, and it can only be comprehended by a knowledge of the life, the thoughts, the habits, and the desires of the people, acquired by an investigation alike profound as it is rare.

The destiny of a nation cannot be forecast and its civic phenomena adequately explained from experience touching the abuse of one privilege, the failure of one system, or the wrongdoing of one class. The study of the effect of a system in the city, with its peculiar relations to the body politic, will not suffice as the foundation of an opinion as to the country at large. The study is too narrow. Rather, to control the thought, and direct our hope, there should be a study of those eternal principles which are deep in the very spirit and breath of the people and which alone guide the destiny of a nation. I repeat that this experience can only arise from a wide study of the people itself. Appreciating those who love the books and respecting "that wit of wisdom," still the highest essential in investigating the people is that rare combination of mind and experience which can both touch elbows with the thought of the people and deduce therefrom a right conclusion. I have in my mind a book of a teacher of youth, who, had he lived in the Athenian days, would surely have owed a cock to Asclepius, wherein, with the authority of high place, he teaches the youth that the majority of those who predominate in the exercise of universal suffrage are vicious and ignorant and prefer the gambling den, the brothel, the saloon, and the prize ring to the exercise of pure politics. Sir, such deductions, their foundations untrue in fact and defective in investigation, lower the moral tone of the student and dishonor the citizens of the Republic. Against such teachings, in the name of the millions of clean-hearted and pure-breathed men whose eyes never beheld the gilding of the saloon and whose souls never knew the infection of the brothel, and who, whilst the furniture may be scanty and the floors bare, hallow the rented house with the unspeakable glory of an honest, pure, and independent citizenship, whose hands, though hardened with work, would spurn the touch of unearned gold, and whose hope and ambition is to leave to their children that same incorruptible citizenship bequeathed to them by the Fathers of the Republic, and in the name of the youth of our country, whose minds are corrupted by such teachings, I enter my earnest protest and dissent. To those who discuss without kindliness or moderation

the great problems of our national existence, I beg
that from the poet of darkened Persia they will read
that lesson of moderation which they have failed to
grasp under a century of free government :

" And Abraham sat in the door of his tent about the
going down of the sun.

" And behold, a man bowed with age came from the
way of the wilderness, leaning on a staff.

" And Abraham arose and met him, and said, Turn
in, I pray thee, and Abraham baked unleavened bread
and they did eat.

" And when Abraham saw that the man blessed
not God, he said unto him, Wherefore dost thou not
worship the most high God, Creator of heaven and
earth ?

" And the man answered and said, I do not worship
the God thou speakest of, neither do I call upon his
name.

" And Abraham's zeal was kindled against the man,
and he arose and drove him forth with blows into the
wilderness.

" And, at midnight, God called upon Abraham,
saying, Abraham, where is the stranger ?

" And Abraham answered and said, Lord, he would
not worship thee, neither would he call upon thy name,
therefore I have driven him out before my face into
the wilderness.

" And God said, Have I borne with him these
hundred ninety and eight years, and clothed him,

notwithstanding his rebellion against me, and couldst not thou, that art thyself a sinner, bear with him one night?

"And Abraham said, Let not the anger of the Lord wax hot against his servant, for lo I have sinned, forgive me, I pray thee.

"And Abraham arose and went forth into the wilderness, and returned with the man to the tent, and when he had entreated him kindly, he sent him away on the morrow with gifts."

Those who look with doubt and uncertainty upon our future remind me that the spirit of democracy in our country is weakening the foundations of home, and is dimming the light which touches, with the glory of holiness, the marital bed. I am not invading the realm of sociology. The purity of the people is the foundation of the civil life of the Republic. It is the very foundation of our political existence. To prove the tendencies towards the increasing laxity of our civil life under the democracy of the day, I am confronted with statistics showing the increase of divorces. Sir, I understand not the jargon of statistics, nor do I trust their rigid conclusions when they conflict with the experiences of my daily life. To believe them is to believe that the veil of the temple has surely been rent in twain and the sacred homes of the people have been filled with "Gorgons, Hydras, and Chimeras dire." I deny the foul aspersion. I have lived my life with the people of the mountains and the country.

Here the vast bulk of the population live. Here, beside the streams, and on the majestic plains, and in the mountains, is the fate of the Republic. By the streams and in the mountains in all the days has God talked with the people, and here, away from the hurry of the city, is the place for the true contemplation of these vital questions of the Republic. No statistical measuring-rod can reach the homes of the people. Sir, in my lifetime I have seen the whole order of life changed, and by the thunderous tramp of your legions in blue our Southern civilization was shaken to ruin. Amid its wreck and revolution, sundered from every tie except that of the little ones, with a guard as of the fiery Cherubim warning her away from the gates of home, alone the mother and wife of the South was touched by no change or revolution. Turning calmly without a sigh from the gentleness of home, she gave herself to the higher, sweeter, and better life, and her nature has not lost its purity and gentleness, nor has her soul been touched or hurt with the hardness of life. Despite casuist and statistician, above the glory of man's effort and success, more potent than power or prestige, there is one spirit untouched, and that is the central figure of American life, the wife and the mother of the American home. To-night, under the stars when the day is done, if, with noiseless fingers, we could touch the veil of the temple in the homes of the people,

" Those everlasting gardens,
     Where angels walk and the seraphs are the wardens,"

we would behold the mother, pure and unspotted,
gathering to her knees the little ones, white robed and
clean, and we would hear, like incense, ascending to
the open gates, from the prairie and the mountain, and
from mansion house and farm and city, over the borders
of this mighty Republic, from the myriads of homes,
the sweetest prayer ever murmured by worshipping
lips:

> " Now I lay me down to sleep,
> I pray the Lord my soul to keep;
> If I should die before I wake,
> I pray the Lord my soul to take."

Here still dwells the immortality of the Republic,
with its plenitude of pure civil life, and surely here
lives, in ancient vigor, the true spirit of our greatness.
In the homes of our Republic is our hope of civil
immortality, and that hope rises triumphant over all
difficulties and complications. For around their sacred
portals lingers the golden sunshine, which is perennial,
and whose splendor is not dimmed by the march of the
day. No, sir, the spirit of democracy has crowned the
head of the American home with an increasing manli-
ness known in no other country under the sun, and
has touched the life of his helpmate with a spirit of
virtue and gentleness which grows in its marvellous
beauty as the years march along.

It is stated with all the power of authority that one
of the tendencies of universal suffrage has been to increase the power of party and to render political strife

more acute, and thus make party more dangerous to the Republic. Is this our experience? It seems to me that the result of the exercise of universal suffrage has been to cause more independence of party and more moderation than ever before. I appeal, Sir, to the facts. In the last election, whose mighty throbs we still feel, there was a greater "scratching" of ballots than ever before known in the history of this government. The Independent in politics has largely been the growth of the last quarter of a century. A careful investigation of the ballots, an examination of the ballot commissioners, and an analysis of the vote in ten separate States, disclose, as never before, the gradual disenthrallment of the voter from party. I call your attention to another statement which, but to mention, carries with it this conclusion. There was never before in your experience or in mine a time when the independent voter was so important and so absolutely Independent. Aye, more than this, there has never been a period since this country was divided by well-defined parties when a man could, with so much equanimity and with as little criticism, turn his back upon his party and upon all of his political traditions as to-day. The protest against the corruption of the day is growing in character and power as never before. In the South, where politics is a passion and where party fealty is of the first importance, the Independent in politics is the greatest political phenomenon of our time. Consider this question somewhat more broadly than in relation to the mere voter. Look for a moment at the attitude of the press to party. We have seen within six years dozens of great newspapers of the country break away from party affiliation. The country within the last ten years has been filled with political clubs and associations, growing in power and importance, with independence of party as the sole reason for their existence. With the rise of these powerful associations has marched the magazine and newspaper, entirely independent as to political control, and reserving the right to criticise or to oppose party.

What has been the tendency of the day under this system in reference to the acerbity and virulence of party politics? Under the existence of universal suffrage the trend of sentiment has been distinctly towards moderation. The scandals, the hatred, the vilification, and the rancor of the old days of the Republic are to-day almost unheard of and would not be tolerated. Let us, for a moment, turn for proof to the past and listen to the turbulent sounds from the golden days of the Republic. Says Mr. Jefferson, " You and I have formerly seen warm debates and high political passions. But gentlemen of different politics would then speak to each other and separate the business of the Senate from that of society. It is not so now. Men who have been intimate all their lives cross the street to avoid meeting and turn their heads another way lest they should be obliged to touch their hats.''

⌣ De Tocqueville quotes the language of the first newspaper upon which his eyes fell when he arrived in this country, and the expression therein contained concerning the President would not to-day be tolerated. Contrast this with the American experience of a great Englishman of to-day. Says Professor Bryce : " Partisans are reckless, but the mass of the people lends itself less to acrid partisanship than it did in the time of Jackson, or in those first days of the Republic, which were so long looked back to as a sort of heroic age. Public opinion grows more temperate, more mellow, and assuredly more tolerant. Its very strength disposes it to bear with opposition or remonstrance. It respects itself too much to wish to silence any voice."

An authority of this city teaches that under our system of universal suffrage the people are losing their love of the united country, and that the bonds binding us together are loosening. Sir, this cannot be the tendency of to-day. Will you allow an illustration to the contrary from my own experience?

Sir, I recall the days of the sorrow of the South, and I well remember, when I stood by the open grave of a Southern soldier. Our armies had been overwhelmed, Virginia was invaded and ruined, and our hope was gone. War, ruthless and unsparing, and Desolation, grim and terrible, galloped booted and ready over the once fair land, and Death, their ever-present handmaiden, filled the hills with sorrow. The green grass was under the mire of the hoof-beat, and the hope of

food for the women and little ones was as blasted as
the white poverty of the fields. Only the cedar and
the pine wore their dresses of green as if to touch the
despair of the present with a tinge of the hope of the
future. To the little group of women and children and
aged men the habiliments of woe prescribed by custom
were not, for war even denied to those who mourned
that gentle clinging to those who had gone as expressed
by the outward tokens of sorrow. Here, an old bit of
black lace ; there, a worn piece of crêpe, a black belt,
a faded hat, mute evidences of the desire to make that
show hallowed by our custom and love, only too
plainly evidenced that grief and ruin had in this devoted land touched their strong hands. Lifting his
eyes to the skies, which alone were bright, the aged
man of God read the wail of the Jews in a foreign land :

" By the rivers of Babylon, there we sat down ; yea,
we wept when we remembered Zion.

" We hanged our harps upon the willows in the
midst thereof.

" For there they that carried us away captive required of us a song ; and they that wasted us required
of us mirth, saying, Sing us one of the songs of Zion.

" How shall we sing the Lord's song in a strange
land ? "

When the ripening harvest was casting its glory of
yellow grain over our renewed land, verily a fair land
bursting with plenty and happiness, within this year,
standing by a soldier's grave, once the wailing place

of a conquered people, I listened to a great son of the North, our honored guest, once a soldier in blue, once our enemy, speaking in burning words to the listening soldiers of Robert E. Lee and Stonewall Jackson, telling them of the glory of this Union, hallowed by our sufferings and sorrow, and doubly blest with the love and peace and happiness of the people. Yea, sir,

> "Hands are clasped in joy unspeakable,
>   Old sorrows are forgotten now,
>   Or but remembered to make sweet the hour
>   That overpays them; wounded hearts that bled
>   Or broke are healed forever."

When I have witnessed this most exceeding love, then forsooth there must be needed something more potent than statistics marshalled under a midnight lamp to convince me that new influences arising from the political system of to-day can impair the peaceful though secret bonds of love binding together the soul and life of this great and free people.

A fierce indictment against universal suffrage is that it accentuates and intensifies the tyranny of the majority. The Fathers did not so fear this tyranny, and they had before them the disturbing ideas of the French Democracy. Mr. Jefferson, in his enumeration of the essential principles to be observed by the people, places among the first as most sacred that "absolute acquiescence in the decisions of the majority the vital principle of Republics from which there is no appeal but to force, the vital principle and immediate parent of despotism.'' But, sir, do we have in the Republic the tyranny of the majority? Filled with the fundamental ideas of the Fathers, and permeated with the genius of free government, this has been a government where the decrees of the majority become the potent will of the whole people. Here is the essential difference between our institutions of free government and the fierce dictatorships of Southern and Central America masquerading under the fair guise of free government. Here the principles of the majority are assimilated and carried to fruition by the whole people. Whilst this is the theory and practice of our government, yet the people have wisely conceived the idea that, whilst they acquiesce in the controlling will of the majority, yet that the theory of the majority should be worked out by the practical assistance of the minority. Hence, with universal suffrage was born the theory of minority representation, and it has grown as part of its life and being. This is the creation of the last half century, and again it is the people protecting against themselves. The desire to preserve the rights of the minority has grown with the people in representative and district elections, and its principle is practically adopted to-day in the State and National Government in the exercise of minority representation on every important governmental board and state institution. Its handmaiden, Civil Service Reform, although suffering the delays incident to all reforms, has taken away one of the most potent criticisms against the rule of the people, and is day by day making fitness and qualification the essentials of place in the government. The rapid extension of this salutary principle, under the rule of, and accentuated by, the free suffrage of the people, is gradually but surely removing any danger to the Republic from the tyranny of the majority.

I would be false to the spirit which brought me here were I to say there are no dangers and no fears in the tendencies of the Democracy. Sir, there are dangers. There are tendencies which excite the apprehension, if not the fear, of those who love the Republic and hallow its faiths and ancestral truths. When there are no fears and no apprehensions in this free government, the world will again witness a people which only wants bread and the games, and whose genius is emasculated and whose vitality is stagnant. The people are meeting the vital questions arising from the relations of the State to the General Government and the equally important question of the citizen's relation to the State, and will solve these epochs wisely for free government.

There is to-day arising an era or epoch in our national life of far more reaching importance than either of the others. These epochs must arise in popular government. In aristocracies and monarchies the strong, central, guiding hand holds the government in the channel and on the quiet sea; and whilst the ship of state does not rock, yet it makes less progress than when driven by the vigorous strength of a whole people.

An era arises insidiously, and in its womb, hidden from the people, are the seeds of disaster and death to popular liberty. Its tendency must be grasped by a people, and its progress stopped, or it will become inherent and the epoch will burst its bounds and the Rubicon will have been passed dividing the people from its liberties. The tendencies of an epoch touching the State, guarded by written constitutional limitations, such as the relation of the citizen to the State, or the relation of the States to the General Government, can be watched. The infraction of this class of rights cannot be insidious. The written law is engraved alike on the brazen posts as well as on the hearts of the people, and the approach of danger can be seen by all men. The epoch or tendency to be dreaded, as containing the very seeds of death to the institutions of a free people, is the era carrying with it the hidden dangers involving the division of the people into classes, the changing of the relations of the people to themselves, the change of sentiment as to the ideas of government, and the corruption of the moral tissues and life of the people resulting therefrom. Here, Sir, is the era of danger to a free people, for it is insidious in its approach, and the rights impinged upon are not written.

Read the history of free government in all ages and in all lands, and from all comes the melancholy message that free government has always been destroyed from within and never from without. It is one broad, marked, unvarying path—a young people filled with freedom, simple, economical, patriotic, the widening of its power, ships on the seas, luxury at home, and influence abroad, privileges for some, discontent for others, the rich and the poor, a Cleon haranguing the people and a Cæsar at the Capital. A tyro can write the simple story. It seems to me that this epoch of our civil life, when the people have largely passed the constructive and creative stages of the nation's existence, when the great fundamental questions of government have been settled, and the people are practically engaged upon these matters which shape for all time the texture and mold of the individual and class relation and existence, is the most important to us and to mankind.

The epoch of to-day into which the people are passing is the era of Commercialism. Its relation is most important to the question under discussion. Sir, with homage for its power, do I mention the spirit of American Commercialism impelled by the restless genius of this people. The Hanging Gardens would be but a plaything of a day for one of our merchant princes, and all the wealth of Rome garnered from Asia Minor and Gaul and Egypt and all of the tribute lands would not suffice to supply for one year the needs of the kings of American commerce. Never was there such power. It has surrounded this continent as a maiden by her girdle. It has pervaded every class. It has turned its eyes to the world, and has grasped in its strong hands the whole universe. It has flung France aside from its path as a puny child. It has stridden past Germany, has throttled England, and stands to-day beside the only power, its comparative equal in future commercial rule, Imperial Russia. It is building bridges in Africa to bear the tramp of the British legions. Its rail to-night lies under the snows of Siberia, and behind its engines are heard the strange mutterings of the bearded Cossack and fierce Ukranian. It is clothing the Celestial in cotton, and it is cutting the bearded wheat in Argentina. Strange tongues are whispering over its cables strung under strange seas. It is selling knives in Sheffield and cloth in France, and is lending money to London. It builds warships for the Czar and sewing-machines for Japan. It digs coal under the winds of Magellan, and gold and diamonds in Africa. Its ships gather commerce from every port, and it buys and sells in every land. It waits not on steam and sail, but shakes the continent in its impatient hands that the waters of the Orient and Occident may flow together to do its bidding. It is omnipresent and almost omnipotent. Was there ever such power? It tosses millions as the boy flips the marble at his play, and its colossal combinations of wealth touch with their golden fingers every useful thing. This unprecedented growth of commercial life, necessarily expressing itself through corporate existence, the growth of interstate commerce, the building and operation of the railroad, the telegraph, and the telephone, and the various wonderful and far-reaching combinations, demanding immediate results to be effective, necessarily restive at all interference, all being the expression of the commercialism of the day, affecting every condition of individual, social, national, and commercial life, demands, as never before, the preservation of that essence of our national life and being, the spirit of American democracy, in all of its mighty strength and unshorn of any of its power.

Now, sir, do not understand me in the slightest degree to underestimate the power for good possessed by wealth. I make my obeisance to the great desire on the part of wealth to send light where there is darkness, to touch the sick and the helpless with soothing care, and to erect on the broadest foundation its monument to learning and the arts. This is a commercial nation, and the desire and power to acquire and use wealth within its legitimate bounds is to be honored by every good citizen. What, then, are the dangers of commercialism? What are its tendencies? Can these tendencies, if dangerous to the Republic, be eliminated by the reimposition of a restrictive franchise? The danger to the Republic from this era is that the legitimate spirit of commercialism will become political commercialism. It is rapidly so becoming. I submit, sir, that this epoch of political commercialism, if unchecked in its tendencies, will destroy the true ideal of the Republic. In our natural haste to grasp and utilize the marvellous material conditions vouch-

safed to us by a new continent, we are losing sight
of the republican principles inculcating those high
and noble virtues which attended the birth of the Republic and which should live as its very texture. The
love of the welfare of the whole people, the wealth of
patriotism, that pride of high character of those in high
places, that jealous desire for an exalted ideal for the
nation, that thorough knowledge of the aims of the
government looking not alone to self-utilization, seem
to me to be lessening under the fierce assault of those
conditions which allow the citizen to such a vast extent
to better his material welfare. It will surely beget a
lower standard of civil life and desire. It is weakening
the true spirit of democracy. Under the spirit as well
as the letter of our institutions we can have no patent
of nobility, but have we not established a class with
success in accumulation as its real patent of nobility?
Are we not making the standard of our ideal of citizenship, that of breadth of acres and numbers of stocks
and wealth of possessions, rather than that of statesmanship, profound learning, exalted patriotism, and
unselfish citizenship? Would not the people to-day
prefer Themistocles rather than listen to Aristides; and
with the dominance of this spirit, so variant from the
true idea of democracy, would not Jove soon fill the
other urn with disastrous fulness. The real spirit of
democracy has been tumbling empires, and overthrow-
ing kingdoms, and lifting the peoples of the world to a
better and higher condition of life. Would not a change

in its very life and texture bereave it of its real glory
and power? Oh, my country,

> "If thou do'st consent
>   To this most cruel act, do but despair;
>   And if thou want'st a cord, the smallest thread
>   That spider ever twisted from her womb
>   Will serve to strangle thee."

The true ideal of democracy as exemplified by this
government is to bear to the world the sublime message
of help, and implant in the heart of the nations the
spirit of hope of freedom and of improvement in every
condition, social and governmental. Are we not changing the true spirit of this high ideal and giving to the
world the message of almost infinite material power, of
ability to trade and hold with the strong hand and
nothing more? I was looking once at a statue of
Hercules, chiselled by a forgotten hand. It was different
from all others I had ever seen and represented the
ideal of my country. High intelligence beamed from
its lofty brow and cultured features; withal it was
strong and powerful, yet its strength was graced by
beauty and activity. Nearby was the old ideal which
we knew so well, thews of brass, a jaw of iron, and
the lowering brow, the idealization alone of unmixed
power. Are we not nearing this ideal of national life?
Do not, I pray you, Mr. Chairman, think me wanting
in the feeling of hospitality or in that spirit of high
appreciation of your courtesy, or that I am filled with
an impossible spirit of knight-errantry, when I stand

here in the heart of this imperial market-place and discuss commercialism. But, sir, I am profoundly impressed with the dangers of this tendency, and I would be recreant to my duty to my country and disingenuous to those who are here seeking for the truth, were I to dissemble or palter with this most vital question of our national life.

This spirit has been the tendency of all the ages, and the broad highway of the world is strewn with the whitened bones of the nations which traversed the fundamental ideas controlling their creation and life. With this tendency so potent and so plain, and arising almost universally from the higher and powerful classes, should we take the tremendous risk of in anywise interfering with the power in the hands of the masses of the people? Should we at this time lay our hands on the real corrective of this tendency which lies within the plainer and poorer people?

Sir, this spirit of commercialism, acting through vast aggregations, must have power, inordinate power. The attainment of some great selfish purpose, the settlement of some commercial principle, the procuring of a franchise belonging to the people, the levying of taxes in one or another form, the obtaining of some special class privilege, the lifting of a burden from one shoulder to be placed upon another, are but a few illustrations of the growing power which has not in view the liberty or the good of the people, but only looks to selfish ends. Then, sir, from this spirit arises that appalling corruption which has spread its powerful influence over this country and which is to-day the chief danger to democratic institutions.

The fathers of this government, with the prescience which characterized their formulation of its principles, understood that the danger to a free government lay in the corruption of the body politic. It is but a truism to again reiterate this fear on the part of the fathers. They discounted every great tendency of the democracy, and in the formulation of their governmental principles arranged to counteract these tendencies. There have been no unforeseen tendencies of the democracy. Yet, sir, they never for a moment understood the vast influences of commercialism which have been sown like the fabled dragons' teeth over the fields of the people. Let us here to-day be plain with each other. The trouble with the higher classes of the American people has been that they have not been ingenuous in dealing with this great question. It is remarkable, but it is true, that anything that concerns the commercial life of the people is touched tenderly by the intelligent classes. It seems to me that the tendency of the democracy demands plain speaking on the part of those who are interested in the immortality of our free institutions. The Republic is in danger. From what source does the corruption spring, Mr. Chairman? Consider the machinery of a national campaign of to-day and you will have the answer. What is its chief burden? To formulate great principles touching the domestic, the national, and international policies of the government? No, sir; it is to raise vast sums of money. For what purpose? It would be cowardice for me to state that these enormous sums are for any purpose other than for the ultimate corruption of the people. Even with the teeming millions of our country these sums could not be legitimately spent. Who contributes them? The plain people, forsooth? Not a dollar! It comes by the thousands and the hundreds of thousands from those who expect to control the governmental policies of the country. Through this power, and we are not now considering the tremendous potentialities of the great vested influences in active operation upon the body politic, do we see the spirit of political commercialism having its dire effect upon the people. It bestrides both the parties like a colossus, and demands from your Congress and your Legislatures the price of its contribution. We are told that this interest in politics is solely for protection. In some instances such is the case. But in the more frequent instances the commercial interest is fiercely aggressive and demands from Congress and Legislature some higher tariff or lower tax or special privilege. It is true, sir, that the great vested interests of this country are often threatened by the demagogue, but only infrequently does he have any practical effect upon legislation or upon the control of affairs. We are frightened with the cry of agrarianism and the enactment of laws against fair treatment of vested interests;

but, sir, I can count on the fingers of one hand the
States where the people have passed laws unjustly discriminating against the great commercial interests of
this country. Says a great authority: "In no country
in the world is property as secure as it is with us. The
guarantees of a constitution now, Mr. Bancroft tells us,
the oldest in Christendom, have intrenched it against
public as well as private attack. The British Parliament during the last half of the century has destroyed
vested rights, broken up titles, seized private property
for private use, in a way that to an American seems
almost revolutionary."

Mr. Bryce observes that bribery does not directly
touch the people. To differ with Mr. Bryce is to
invite most serious controversy. The condition of
to-day, however, shows the fell progress of corruption.
I have seen the shambles of corruption, filled with
money from high places, opened wide and with scarcely
a pretence of concealment until the outraged decency
of the plain people rebelled. I speak earnestly, because
it is the vital question of our national life, whether or
not the ballot-box, the sacred custodian of the liberties
of the people, reflects the unbiassed and unpurchased
opinion of the people. From this spirit of corruption
arise the Machine and the Boss, for without money
and its attending sinister influences they cannot live in
the pure air of our free institutions. What I am attempting to inculcate is that political immorality comes
not from the plain people, but most largely from the

influences dominated by the higher class, which class cannot be reached by the reimposition of a franchise limitation.

How change these tendencies? How guide the mighty river so that its flood may fructify the earth and all of its peoples? The tendencies towards evil are not yet flowing with the blood and do not yet inhere into the bone of the people. This change cannot be accomplished by Courts of Impeachment and Removal, the Referendum, the Electoral Delegates, and the thousand nostrums which are the mere modifications of the machinery of government, unaccompanied by the pure controlling spirit of popular life. These slight erections would soon be engulfed in the waves of a shoreless democracy. It would be binding the tide with ropes. The remedy must be deeper. Would these tendencies be changed by the reimposition of a suffrage limitation? You could not impose a money or a property qualification. An educational or an intelligence qualification would only be considered by the people.

Would the imposition of an intelligence franchise affect the general status? A few brief illustrations will show beyond cavil that an intelligence franchise, outside of the Southern States, where, by reason of the large illiterate negro vote, the conditions are abnormal, will not affect the general tendency. Let us illustrate by the States in this Union which have more than others felt the effect of political corruption. Take the

States of New York, Pennsylvania, Ohio, and Illinois. These have been pivotal States and they have been swamped with money, and it is interesting to consider the effect of the illiterate vote. The total population of New York State at the census of 1890 was 4,822,392. The number of illiterates was 266,911, or 5.5 per cent. of the whole population. Estimating one vote to every four of population, there were, in round numbers, 1,205,000 voters, and 66,000 illiterate voters. Considering one-third of these illiterate voters to be venal, which is a large proportion, there would be in New York State 22,000 corruptible voters, through illiteracy, or one and five-sixths per cent. of the whole voting population, which would be reached by the imposition of the franchise regulation and thus debarred from political life. This leaves the question of the effect of 22,000 venal voters upon practically a million and a quarter of intelligent voters. Would it account for the great corruption which is alleged to exist in New York State? This proportion does not even hold good at this period, for the illiterate vote is rapidly decreasing throughout the country. In the period between 1870 and 1890 the illiteracy in New York State decreased from 7.1 per cent. to 5.5 per cent. In that proportion of decrease the danger of the vote arising from illiteracy in New York State would be decreased to about one per cent. of the whole voting population, or, in round numbers, to about 15,000 votes of her voting population of about one and one-half millions.

In this regard let us consider New York City. There were 38,420 of illiterate males over ten years of age in 1890. Of these we will say that there were 35,000 voters. Allowing one-third of these to be considered as venal through illiteracy, we will have about 11,500 dangerous voters through illiteracy in the whole population of 1,210,000, or less than one per cent. of the whole population of the city.

The population in Pennsylvania in 1890 was 4,063,134. Its illiterate population was 275,353, or 6.8 per cent. of the whole population. Its voting population was 1,015,000, and the illiterate voting population was, in round numbers, 68,000. Allowing one-third to be corruptible, can we account for the debauchery of Pennsylvania politics by the presence of 23,946 who are corruptible through illiteracy out of a voting population of over 1,000,000? So with Illinois, with its voting population of 726,918, and its illiterate voting population of 38,158. Considering 12,719 of these to be venal, would that affect the virtue of the remaining three-quarters of a million of honest voters? Ohio teaches the same lesson in almost identical figures. Iowa, with only 3.6 per cent. illiterates in the whole population, should certainly not feel the effect of its illiterate vote of a little more than four thousand upon its whole voting population.

There are other States where the rate of illiteracy is much higher, but what is remarkable is the fact that, with possibly two exceptions, in those States the corruptible element is smaller than in the States where the illiteracy is proportionately much less.

The lesson of these figures is potent, and shows, beyond any question, that the imposition of the intelligence franchise would reach only a very small portion of the vote considered venal, and that the illiterate vote, even if we consider the whole of it venal, would have comparatively small effect, moral or otherwise, upon the total voting population. This vote, comparatively infinitesimal in numbers and unimportant by reason of its ignorance, further loses its power for evil, for it has no cohesiveness, and its strength is dissipated between the parties.

More than this, my experience for years has been that the man peculiarly susceptible to corruption is not the one who cannot read and write. The potent elements of corruption are, primarily, the classes which provide the means for corruption, and, secondly, the agents whom they employ to use them. These can always read and write. The mere mechanical power to read and write, add and subtract, will surely not affect a man's political honesty, nor will it make a revolution in the sentiment of the people. Some more potent corrective to corruption is surely needed. You must educate the souls and the lives of the people with a higher and better education than that imparted by the knowledge of a few elementary books. This education must reach their love of country and envelop the people with a nobler and a grander and purer ideal of citizenship. What is needed is an education of their citizenship, not a mere education of the mind. This is the only education which can reach the crisis of to-day. More than this, will not the rapidly decreasing illiteracy resulting from our system of education soon destroy the necessity for an intelligence qualification for the franchise ?

Above these considerations there is a higher and more potent objection to the reimposition of the franchise limitation. This objection touches the very heart of the nation's being. It will be turning our lives against the advance of modern political science. The sovereignty of the whole people is the dominant, aggressive, and vital principle of to-day throughout the world. It has made a democracy of England and a republic of France. Its spirit jostles the soldiers in Berlin, and it controls monarchical Europe. It shakes the Czar sitting on the only despotic throne in civilization. This spirit was born with our Republic, and should we be the power to arrest its development throughout the nations of the world? Would it not fix the attention of civilization upon class as the model we give it upon which to rebuild the institutions of government? Shall we bind the hands of this potent spirit and say to the people of the world, struggling against king and emperor and class and privilege, that the fundamental theory of our government is at fault, and that the people cannot be entirely trusted? Could we, in justice to our theory of government, send this message to the world after a hundred years of our civilizing free government? Shall we place Chinese shoes on American feet and put the American citizen in a Procrustean bed? Would it not be an unhappy lesson for free government? Should we not rather take lessons from our old mother England? With a limited franchise, her elections were corrupt, and her administrative abuses were enormous. With a gradual change in her franchise to an almost universal suffrage, we behold corruption practically abolished and governmental abuses almost unknown. Verily, the remedy must be deeper. Sir, there must be reform, and it must come from the higher classes. It must be a true reform of the people, and not in the mere machinery of suffrage. The protest against the tendencies of the day must begin with you and me, and its action must be continuous and not ephemeral. It must not be a crusade, but should be a part of our lives. It should not express itself by a sermon once a year, illustrated by a trip to the slums under the protection of a policeman; but the inculcation of high political morals should be part and parcel of our everyday work and teachings of the church. We must demand that those in control of the affairs of commercial influences shall keep their hands away from the people, and by precept and example sternly enforce that demand. The pruning of the political tree must begin at the top and not at the root. The danger to the Republic is not to-day to be feared from the lower classes.

14

The intelligent and critical classes who are not interested in some governmental policy for personal purposes have left the practical control of political affairs to the other classes of the body politic. This is essentially a political nation, and if the intelligent and disinterested citizen does not interest himself in governmental affairs either those interested for selfish purposes or the ignorant will take control. This government, while a free government, will not run itself. It is founded upon the joint exertion of all of its citizens and not alone on the efforts of the corner grocery man and the place hunter. The people are guided by intelligence ; and the disinterested and intelligent classes in this country, if they will but interest themselves in political affairs, will be the great potential factors in our political life. I repeat that the corrective influence must begin work in its own class and enforce its demand for pure government. It will surely succeed, for the people will earnestly respond to the demand of the disinterested and intelligent citizen. This government is founded upon the people. I believe in the people and they love this government and revere its abiding principles. They believe in the permanency of our free institutions. They love the Constitution, and whilst in moments of haste and passion they may wander, yet surely will they return to the vital principles of popular government. An honest appeal to the patriotism of the people has never yet by them been disregarded. The reform of mere political machinery will not suffice for this critical epoch in our governmental affairs. The people must again be summoned to their tents, the rich and the poor, the learned and the unlearned, abiding together as of old, and the palladium of our faith, which has ever guided us in all our wanderings, must be again brought to our view. Hear again the law and listen to the real hope for the correction of the wrong tendencies of the Democracy :

"Equal and exact justice to all men of whatever state or persuasion, religious or political ; peace, commerce, and honest friendship with all nations, entangling alliances with none ; the support of the State governments in all their rights, as the most competent administrations of our domestic concerns and the surest bulwarks against anti-republican tendencies ; the preservation of the General Government in its whole constitutional vigor, as a sheet-anchor of our peace at home and safety abroad ; a jealous care of the right of election by the people ; a mild and safe correction of abuses, which are lopped by the sword of revolution, when peaceable remedies are unprovided ; absolute acquiescence in the decisions of the majority, the vital principle of republics, from which there is no appeal but to force, the vital principle and immediate parent of despotism ; a well disciplined militia, our best reliance in peace, and for the first moments in war, till regulars can relieve them ; the supremacy of the civil over the military authority ; economy in the public expense, that labor may be lightly burdened ; the honest payment of our debts, and sacred preservation of the public faith ; encouragement of agriculture, and of commerce as its handmaid ; the diffusion of information, and arraignment of all abuses at the bar of the public reason ; freedom of religion, freedom of the press, freedom of person under the protection of the Habeas Corpus ; and trial by juries impartially selected.''

Sir, with the earnestness of one who loves the Republic, I believe that if we will grasp the people more closely to us in the bonds of a common patriotism, show them an example of high political morality among the intelligent and powerful, place before them the ancestral faiths as the texture of our national being, touch arms and hearts with them as part and parcel of the common body politic, public sentiment will become more lofty, patriotism will be revived and made more holy, and without touching limb or twig of its mighty power, democracy will be disenthralled from the tendencies which disturb the day. These alone, sir, are the mighty agents which will dethrone the Boss, break the Machine, correct abuses, and touch again with life the altars of the country where deep down in the hearts of the people the fires of patriotism are burning clear and true. Will this save the Republic? That it will, I again summon as witness the mighty spirit of him from whose heart and hand were born the words and spirit of our Constitution. "These principles," says the Father of the Constitution, "form the bright constellation that has gone before and guided our steps through an age of revolution and reformation. They should be the creed of our political faith, the text of civic instruction, the touchstone by which to try the services of those we trust. And should we wander from them in moments of error and alarm, let us hasten to retrace our steps and to regain the road which alone leads to peace, liberty, and safety.''

The witnesses are about us to-night that these words are as true to-day as they were in the springtime of the Republic. The splendor of this presence of the learned, the great, and the powerful within the gates of this imperial city, listening to the words of a plain mountain man as he tells of the simple faiths of the Republic, fills me with hopes unspeakable for the perpetuity of our free government. Aye, sir, I can bear the message to the plain people of the country that here, amidst the silks and spices, the glitter and power of incomprehensible wealth, the hurry of trade, surrounded by all of the novel concomitants of our civilization, still abide the simple faiths of our ancestors.

In my home, on the banks of a sweet Southern river, under the shadows of the mountains keeping their eternal watch and ward over the men who ceaselessly come and go, in the simple room where I read my books, stands a marble pedestal surmounted by a broken slab of stone. Traced in its brazen binding are the momentous words: ''On this stone, at Montgomery, Alabama, February the eighteenth, 1861, Jefferson Davis was inaugurated President of the Confederate

States of America." By some chance of the books, I found on the broken, worn piece of stone the Life of Abraham Lincoln, and from its white leaves there breathed, as the glory of the fruition of a good man's prayer, louder and clearer than the relic freighted with the precious argosy of our tears, these words of encouragement to those who hope and believe in the immortality of our free institutions: "That government of the people, by the people, for the people, shall not perish from this earth."

And may the Almighty, who has glorified the Republic and blessed its people, in all of the days keep ever present to you of the city your faith in these almost inspired words, for it is of more permanent value to mankind than all the jewels, the gold and the silver, and the houses within your encircling waters.

V

SOME TENDENCIES OF THE DAY

WHEN in a great city, surrounded by all of the concomitants of the material glory of this era, in sight of ships laden for far-off lands, jostled with hurrying crowds filled with the absorbing spirit of the age, I received the courteous note of the distinguished president of your college asking me to be here on this day, it seemed to be redolent with the spirit of the old Virginia and her sacrifices for this country's good. The splendid and self-sacrificing labors of your president for Virginia surely entitles him to call upon her sons to hold up his hands in his earnest and effective work for the re-creation of the glories of the old State. Hoping that we may be touched with the spirit of Virginia life, I am here to discuss, in my humble way, the manner in which we should meet the duties of this important era.

On occasions like this, fraught with such importance to the developing minds and energies of the young men of my country, I would wish for opportunity for that reflection which indulgence from exacting labor alone can give. Such, however, cannot be allowed by the spirit of the day. Our country is building a majestic temple to this era, and it is only when the censers are swinging slowly and the keys of our re-sounding progress are touched for the moment on a minor note, that the humble workman, in the shade of lintel and architrave, even for a time, can allow plummet, trowel, and plane to fall from his busy hands.

In the life of every country, there arrive eras or epochs dominated by the spirit or tendency of the time. These eras take their course, affecting the country for good or for evil, according as their spirit is met by the people. The bad effects of an era are as plainly to be observed upon the habits and thought of a people as the murky waters of a sewer are to be seen discoloring a pellucid stream. If, however, an era is wisely met, its passing leaves a nation tingling with an exalted patriotism. If a nation fails at the crucial time to so meet the bad tendency of an era, it is left struggling with the seeds of disease. These statements are the oft-told tales, the mere truisms of political history, and I will not expend the time, which your partiality has so kindly allotted to me, in discussing other eras of our history ; but, without further delay, we will call to your attention the era of to-day, with its power for good or for evil, and to your tremendous part in preserving its real spirit and glory, and in protecting our institutions from its inherent dangers.

The untold wealth garnered from our fertile land ; the golden incense drifting from the tall towers of our manufactories, flooding new countries, enveloping strange races; the quick grasping within our nervous hands of the paramount commercial interests of the earth; the changing of the seat of the world's exchange, following the sun towards its rest, glorifying in its course Ctesiphon and Byzantium and Venice and Holland and England, and resting for a while in its eternal cycle on the shores of this land closest towards the West, all plainly show that we, in our turn with the other nations, have arrived at our Era of Commercialism.

How preserve the material glory of this era within the limitations imperatively demanded by the traditions and genius of our people? How extend its legitimate power and concurrently preserve this country from a government of utilitarianism, the mere government of wealth and power, with no high ultimate ambition, but with sure culminations in the lessening of the importance and the decay of the higher virtues of the citizen? At the critical period, Rome did not differentiate between the real and higher objects of government and the mere acquisition of naked power and wealth. Hence she failed. She had no class of citizens animated with that high and exalted intelligence where the vital essence of government could be fully preserved. She did not retain the high ideals of citizenship, but fell into the control of iron force and physical power. The result was sure: a Verres in Sicily; the wide swath of proconsular ruin in Africa, in Gaul, and in the East; the ultimate decay of Rome's free institutions; and then "the dark-skinned daughters of Isis, with drum and timbrel and wanton mien ; devotees of the Persian Mithras ; emasculated Asiatics ; priests of Cybele, with their wild dances and discordant cries ; worshippers of the great goddess Diana ; barbarian captives with the rites of Teuton priests ; Syrians, Jews, Chaldean astrologers, and Thessalian sorcerers."

The genius of our civilization will allow to us no turning back in the tide of the world's trade, nor can we change the era of commerce at home. We can only guide the course of these great movements. How guide them is the living, throbbing question of to-day. How change the unvarying rule of history ? How differentiate between the real glory and the inherent dangers of this class of epochs, which of all eras have been the most fateful to the nations of the earth ? Our answer to this riddle of the ages is, that its questions can be solved and the real glory of our institutions perpetuated by jealously preserving the exalted character of American citizenship. The most important element of that character in the citizen is an intelligence which will perceive amidst the grandeur of our material triumphs the hidden dangers to our institutions, and whilst fostering the one will jealously watch the dangers of the other.

The character of an era of commerce is necessarily the most complicated because it is more widely ramified than any other, and demands the highest degree of intelligence to thoroughly comprehend it in its thousand different effects upon the life of the people.

An epoch of war, or an era of governmental creation, administration, or reconstruction, is more easily to be comprehended and its respective dangers can be more readily grasped, because through the skein, tangled though it may be, there is always the one controlling thread. Moreover, these last-mentioned epochs are generally controlled by some master spirit, whose genius has given him supreme control in the exigencies of the era. Some Cavour or Cromwell, towering above his fellows, has understood and firmly grasped the conditions of the hour, and the people have followed the master's guidance. This cannot be in an era of commercialism. This era is the result of the infinite interminglings by the people of their more than infinite interests. It is the development of the elements of a complex civilization with its ramifications, which generally are not understood or perceived. The era of commercialism concerns the whole people. Its spirit laughs with the farmer as the sunshine gathers the fields in its ripening embrace. It ripples with the waters and sings in the sails as the ship, filled with the products of our busy hands, flies to distant lands. It walks in the crowded marts of the cities and touches with its controlling spirit men of every class and condition. It furnishes an open field for our thrift and gratifies us by its independence. It arrives, however, at only one height, and its tendency, unwatched and unguarded, is to measure men and civilizations and governments by its own unchangeable Procrustean rule. It appeals to our love of power and ministers to every comfort. It is all-pervading, and within its rightful bounds it is right. It is a part of the inner life of all the people, and its tendencies cannot be guided or arrested by the spirit of one genius, but can be reached only by rousing the action of all of the people. It is slow-moving and insidious, and to conserve its legitimate glory and arrest its evil tendencies there is needed the highest intelligence of all the body politic.

This imposing spectacle of young and intelligent manhood assembled here, where "we behold the bright countenances of truth in the quiet and still air of delightful studies," is the inspiration of my answer that the mighty questions of this era can be met and solved for the ultimate good of the Republic by the exalted intelligence of American citizenship. And here let me enter my earnest protest against the half-grounded mediocrity which only glances into the outer life of the affairs of to-day. The half-taught man will not suffice for the peculiar needs of the citizenship of this era. That mediocrity of intelligence which will not strive to recognize the high and important and rightful place that material power should hold in this Republic is not fitted to settle the direction of this era. More than this, that mediocrity of intelligence which will not differentiate between making wealth and its influence and its acquirement the standard of all civic excellence, and that radicalism which denies to material power any influence in the body politic, will but increase the dangers of the era. Here will be needed the very sublimity of the intelligence of American citizenship. For whilst energizing and developing the life of this commercial era the citizen of this day must preserve, unimpaired in pristine vigor, the foundations beneath our institutions of liberty. How vast and how splendid will be your opportunity! Consider the field upon which to expend your powers, cultivated and strengthened within this great institution of learning.

Whether for national weal or woe is hidden in the womb of the future, the isolation of our past has flown with the spirit of the day. Every question has broadened in its scope, and our old system of commercial life has changed its very being. " Not rivers and provinces and peoples are implicated, but oceans and continents and races; not parties and policies, but hemispheres and civilizations. The world itself is involved. On the hinge of these questions may turn, is likely to turn, the history of centuries."

The peopling of our fields, the excess of our products beyond our needs, the restless energies of this free people, have overthrown the barriers of sea, distance, and tradition. The West, no longer aglow with the rainbow of promise to the hosts of Europe, but thronged with its own earnest people, has turned its face to the millions of the East, there to fight out on the broadest field of endeavor ever vouchsafed to man the supreme contest for the control of the world's commerce. The gauge of its battle is the broad Pacific, and the fruit of victory is the control of the civilization of five hundred millions of men. To the solemn words of the Father of his Country, that "the great rule of conduct for us in regard to foreign nations is, in extending our commercial relations, to have with them as little political connection as possible," the militant spirit of to-day replies: "It is vain that men talk of keeping free from entanglements. Nature is omnipotent, and nations must float with the tide. Whither the exchanges flow they must follow, and they will follow as long as their vitality endures."

With this marvellous change in the direction of national effort produced by the spirit of the day, I will be pardoned for hurriedly placing before you a small part of the tremendous responsibilities of the American citizen necessarily arising from the spirit of the era, which has propelled him into the very midst of the most crucial and important affairs of the earth.

It will be your duty, with no precedent to guide, to create legislation which will control the life and constitute the government of millions of men of alien race and which will control the destiny of the islands of the Southern Seas. You will be the potent factor in the final arbitration of the living questions of the East, involving the peace of the world.

"We front the sun and on the purple ridges
The Virgin Future lifts her veil of snow."

Along the shores of the Pacific will boil with fervid heat the great caldron of the world's selfishness and greed. Here will meet Anglo-Saxon and Slav, armed *cap-a-pie* for the final contest for the control of the civilization of the world. On this colossal field must be settled the momentous problems involving the open door of commerce to millions of men, the levying of indemnities, the delimitations of spheres of influence, the dismemberment of empires, and the practical conquest and control of nations. Wondrous will be the field of endeavor for the American citizen, and surely his spirit should be filled with the highest ideals of free government. It will be for your strong hands to open wide the closed door of commerce to millions of people that through its lintels may flow the sunlight of Western life and thought, fructifying those strange lands with our conception of a higher and more glorious governmental and individual existence. Alone of the nations desiring no territorial aggrandizement, it will be for you to resist oppression by example and influence, to demand equal and exact justice to Caucasian, Malay, and Mongolian, and to place among far-off peoples a monument whose foundations are based upon the high ideals and broad intelligence of American citizenship.

Holding, as I do, that it is against the policy of our country to further extend politically our boundaries, yet the hour is upon us when we will control the trade, and through that channel dominate the life and governmental policy of every republic on the Western Hemisphere. To still the warring elements and to mould the disturbed commonwealths into models of good government, will surely need the wisest exercise of the genius of our citizenship. With this era upon us, with an opportunity and desire to consummate these exalted ideals of our civilization, in comparison how insignificant and inglorious have been the aims of other nations in their dealings with the peoples of the world—Egypt for war, Venice for trade, Rome for power, and France for military glory.

As we contemplate this epoch, this grasping of the lintels of the globe in the hands of the American civilization, it seems that the vision goes beyond the ken of mortal man. Not since the Great Navigator turned his eyes westward upon our land has there occurred an era with greater power to affect mankind. Here is the broadest civilization of the most powerful and virile people on earth, impelled by forces beyond our comprehension, pouring its life upon the teeming millions of the East. In this solemn hour, when you are booted and spurred and ready to face this crisis in your country's life and this epoch in the world's history, I implore you to cherish in your inmost heart the true ideals of the Republic. Here, on this hallowed soil, where the mountains first grew radiant with the flame of our country's shrine, I call to your mind the traditions of our land. I pray that as your eyes look upon the nations you may not alone see the gold and silver and the trappings of material power, and that the hands lifted for truth and light may not be heeded for the flash of the encircling jewel. Holding close to your hearts the traditions of freedom, of right and justice, of the rule of the people under the same law for rich and poor, empires will be shaken, despotism will be dethroned, and justice will be meted out with even hands to the nations of the East. As you stand here with your faces brightened by the radiance of the lands near the rising sun, I would swear you to cling to these principles by an oath more solemn than any ever breathed by gray-clad pilgrim, staff in hand, impatient to walk in the life scenes of the Blessed Master. It was for him alone to bow at a broken tomb and touch with reverent lips a dismantled shrine where the breath of years had winnowed away all save the spirit of other times. With you it is to deal with life and the living, with those who reap and sow; and if you are true to our country's ideals, this era will work out for the world a civilization "beyond which God's divinest secrets lie."

Is there needed more than my rude limnings of the bare outlines of your transcendent duties in this era to nerve you to the grasping of that high intelligence which will enable you and your country to successfully accomplish the work which in God's own good time has been made so ready for your hands in other lands and other climes?

When we view our own land, the changes wrought

15

by the era of commerce in our material life are even more far-reaching and important in their enduring effect upon our civic life.   The colossal combinations, revolutionizing the conditions of our commercial being and absolutely starting the very foundations of our country's life; the growth of enormous fortunes denied to kings, enabling their corporate or individual possessors to touch at will every concern in the life of the people; the unparalleled growth of dependence upon material power necessarily resulting therefrom, whilst strengthening the hands of this republic in its majestic march to the material supremacy of the world, yet have brought the people of our country face to face with the most important era, excepting one, which has touched life within the last half century of its existence.

And here I will be pardoned for the assertion of another truism of political history.   It is this—that whilst in the lifetime of every historic people there may appear important eras or cycles, they are often adventitious, that is, they appear in one people and may not appear in another; yet, sure as the return of the flowers of springtime, in the history of every historic people there has appeared the era of commercialism and material power, and its ultimate effect has been hurtful to the country's real inner life.   I do not here discuss whether this is cause or effect.   I found my fears on the inexorable law of nations.   When a nation has arrived at a great height of material splendor and power, its commercial era, it has first paused, then halted, and ere long has fallen aside and listened to the feet of newer peoples beating on the path the music of the oft-recurring cycle. A general deduction from the examples of history may be unscientific, for every conclusion must have its logical premises; yet on the unwinding of the scroll of human affairs, this commercial epoch has always left the nation showing the decay of those splendid moral and mental virtues which made it historic.

I will be pardoned here for a digression in order that I may be clearly understood. We would not arrest the march of the material glory of this era. This people has never faltered when meeting a crisis in its affairs. No hand should curb the legitimate power of the day. He who would seek by legislation or political effect to impair the rightful progress of material power is an enemy of the Republic. We of the South, surrounded by an empire of material wealth such as graces no other portion of the land, would be doubly recreant to our country did we not fashion it into life and power. Under our bright sun, we would create that wealth of material splendor which would hide under its glory all of our sorrows and tears, yet we would hallow its life and power with that elevation ot thought and nobleness of purpose which would be more potent to mankind than the proudest monument ever erected to material power.

To resume, I do not believe that the citizens of this Republic are losing their love for the principles which have given to us conditions of happiness unsurpassed by any country or in any age. These great principles of government unmistakably show their living influence in the life which is widening and broadening the sphere of our commercial and civic existence. With me, there is no pessimism as to the future of the Republic; but the conditions of the day bear with them the inevitable consequence, that as a nation gathers great material power it naturally looks to its influence for safety rather than to the virtue, patriotism, and high character of the citizen, which are the walls of defense of a truly historic and epoch-making people.

A government of the people is the most difficult to keep straight and true on its course; and unless the people, the final repository of all the power, hold firmly to the true underlying principles of citizenship the real glory of a country must surely decay. This government was not founded on the paramount idea of trade and commerce; yet the wisdom of the Fathers recognized that these questions were most important to the new government. They thundered against the King their anathema " for cutting off trade with all parts of the world." Whilst the contest for liberty in England universally arose over the question of taxation, it was, however, a minor portion of the structural scheme of our governmental policy, and was adverted to because the acts complained of constituted an interference with the liberties and personal rights of our people, which they were determined to fully and completely establish.

As Mr. Burke says, trade has been the mere pulse of liberty.

Our government was built on the higher, nobler, and more lasting foundation of the freedom and the rights and the supreme power within the law of the citizen, and the chief thought of the Fathers was directed to the best method of perpetuating those rights. "That no free government or the blessings of liberty can be preserved to any people but by the firm adherence to justice, moderation, temperance, frugality and virtue, and by a frequent recurrence to fundamental principles," was the culminating clause as to these majestic principles voiced by the Bill of Rights of Virginia. Every declaration underlying our policy of government was redolent of the citizen. He was the supreme question of consideration.

With the lessons of years before us, does not every American citizen join us in thunderous acclaim that only upon the broad basis of the preponderating influence of the citizen can free government work out its supreme destiny? I do not apologize for a reiteration of these principles underlying our country's life. I am taught that only by a recurrence to the historic principles of the country can the texture of its life be preserved. Amidst the material glory of this era it is easy to forget them. Surrounded by all of the evidences of this material era, the natural tendency is to regard that material glory as the true end of government. To conserve it against every other interest, and to subordinate the ideals of the Republic to its interests, is the sure result of the continued contemplation of this side of our civilization. Its splendors become typical of the essence of our life. This result is natural and in consonance with human nature. With the touch of this material era, palaces rise to the skies, cities are crowded by life and action, and the uncounted evidences of material splendor lend their glamour to the spirit of the times.

The material interests thus dominate and control the whole scope of the people's life and government. Hence, ere we realize it, that spirit of republican equity, founded on the citizen and his supreme position in the State, is impaired. This is one of the dangers to our people, resulting from the action of this era of commercialism. The fear that the great co-ordinations of capital, springing armed and equipped from the womb of this era, may impair some of our institutional rights will, I believe, never be realized. These organizations, uncontrolled by wise restrictive law, are hurtful and they may work an injury to our country's life; but I believe that never will they become dangerous to the underlying principles of our government. Their overt attempts to seize unauthorized power can be easily observed, and the citizen of the Republic, alive to that danger, will sternly repress any such inclinations. The danger is in other directions.

The controlling characteristic of the American citizen

has been his spirit of initiative. He has been his own master, asking no assistance, expecting no co-operation beyond that conceded to every man under the laws of the land. He has been supreme in his control of those enterprises to which he has placed his hand. He has leaned on no man, and the success of his endeavor has added measure to the majestic height of his independent citizenship. Under the commercial system of the day, the vast majority of our citizens must depend upon enterprises originated and controlled by others. This will surely impair the self-reliance and sturdy independence of our citizenship.

There is another and more insidious tendency towards danger. The ease of the organization of enormous combinations of capital for the control of the great enterprises of the day, and the greater effectiveness of the corporation over the individual organization, have the invariable tendency to place the citizen in the background, and to minimize and destroy his supreme influence in our policy of government. This tendency is dangerous because it is insidious and gradual. The wisdom, the energy, the supreme power of the citizen has been the propelling influence of the creation of this marvellous material era, and the fear of those who thoughtfully study their country's problems is that the individual citizen, the creator of these material glories, will be dominated by the enormous forces so created. Here is the danger of a revolution in the status of the citizen, more important in its effect

than any which has ever been undergone by our
people. Behind this material power should be the
individual citizen, and if we carry to completion the
tremendous work placed in our hands, his power and
influence must not be foreshortened by one hands-
breadth. His spirit and energy and individuality
must vitalize and dominate these mighty forces. The
citizen is the supreme unit in our material existence.
If we pass out of this era with our country's power
broadened and our national character unimpaired, it
will be alone due to the citizen. Material power was
never interested in the broadening of the rights of the
people. In the evolution of Anglo-Saxon liberty, the
citizen has been the supreme spirit against vested
interest, right or privilege, class and material power.
He looks through the mist of the half-history at
Runnymede. He was at Naseby, Dunbar, and Marston Moor. He was at Lexington, Bunker Hill, Cowpens, and Jamestown. From his brow sprung Magna
Charta, Remonstrance, and Declaration. With the
gaping doors of the Tower wide open, he lighted England with the flame of fire, "that the liberties, franchises, privileges, and jurisdictions of Parliament are
the ancient and undoubted birthrights and inheritance
of the subjects of England."

When we contemplate his real grandeur, his absolute importance in our system of existence, the days
of the tyranny of the Stuarts arise before us. The
old chamber so redolent of the struggle for England's

liberty is filled to-day with anxious faces. At the bar
stand the framers of the illegal tax, refusing to answer
at the Commons, alleging that their acts were at the
command of the King. Protests had been unheeded
and were unavailing, and no wrongs had been re-
dressed. Ere patriot hands had locked the doors, on
their oaken panels thundered the ushers of the King,
demanding admittance to summon the House to the
Lords for final adjournment. We see Pym with his lips
hot with patriot speech : "Our Petition is for the laws
of England, and this power seems to be another power
distinguished from the power of the law." There sat
Coke blaming himself for his timid counsels, which
had prevented Eliot's purpose to propose the Remonstrance. Here was John Hampden: " I could be con-
tent to lend," said he, " but fear to draw on myself
the curse of Magna Charta, which should be read
twice a year against those who infringe it." And
over there was Wentworth, with the shadow of his
apostasy not yet upon him, declaring, "We must
vindicate our liberties ; we must reinforce the laws
of our ancestors ; we must set such a stamp upon
them as no licentious spirit shall hereafter dare
to invade them." And then high above the thunders of the King's servants at the doors, above the
protest of apostate speaker held in his chair by liberty-loving hands, reaching down to us through the
broken corridors of time, come the defiant words
of Sir John Eliot, " None have gone about to break

Parliaments, but in the end Parliaments have broken them."

When we read pages like these from the history of our civilization, it makes our hearts burn with pride at the one great central figure of liberty's progress, the citizen. From scenes like these arises our country's glory; and am I not to be excused for holding out to its young thought the ineffable importance of preserving in all of his power the citizen, the essence, the life and inspiration of our national hope? The law of material power has never changed in the history of the world, and when we summon from the tomb the spectres of nations dead and gone, all will bear for us solemn warning that the true grandeur and permanence of a government cannot be founded alone on material power.

The material glory of the nations was playing its part before the now overthrown columns of hoary Karnak lifted their lotus-crowned heads over the plains of the Nile. It was holding high carousal on the banks of the Euphrates and the Tigris before the deep foundation stones of Babylon and Nineveh and Rome had found their resting-place. Yea, even before the lions of Mycenæ began their ceaseless watch of the gates, it held glorious carnivals amidst the peoples of old. It is an old, old story. Amidst its exultation arose the sweet perfume of the spices of Sheba's queen, and through its halo there spread to the uttermost parts of the ear th the glory of the riches and the wisdom of

King Solomon; yet over the Towers of David, blessed with the smile of the Redeemer of Mankind, there gleam to-day the Crescent and the Cimeter, the insignia of another people, and typical of governmental vice and incapacity. The tramp of its serried legions echoed through the Cilician Gates and beneath the deep shades of the German forests and over the far cities of the East; yet, amidst the fast-enveloping sands of a desolation unspeakable, a ruined gateway surmounted by the imperial eagle still defiantly holding in its broken talons the shattered inscription, "Here the God Terminus rested towards the South," is typical of imperial Rome. This material glory seemed founded on eternal foundations, buttressed by Church and State, when Kings and Pope met and delimited to Portugal and Spain the New World, giving to one the Brazils and to the other the North; yet within the two revolving suns your young eyes have seen the passing of the sail which carried away the shrunken glory of once imperial Spain to be forever locked within the mountains of the Iberian Peninsula. Under its mighty influence pylon and tower and obelisk, walled city and fertile field, attested to the glory of the Babylonish kingdoms; yet the Lord did not more certainly breathe His eternal silence upon the mailed legions of the tented hosts of the Assyrian, than have His hands wrought the desolation of desolations upon their fertile lands, blooming gardens, and towering cities.

The glint of their velvets and the sheen of their silks robbed the sky of its sapphire, its orange, and its blue; yet now, amidst the sand-encumbered columns of Tyre and Sidon, the lonely fisherman mends his broken nets. When we contemplate the immortality of this Republic, there arise before us the stately Parthenon and the blue Ægean hallowed by the glory and letters and patriotism of Athens; and winging over degenerate Greece come the vaulting words of Pericles: "The grandeur of this our Athens causeth the produce of the whole earth to be imported here."

The preservation in this era of the dignity and influence of the citizen, the jealous perpetuation of his aspirations, the real end of our government, can alone write on the scroll of the world's history a new page changing all historic experience and illuminating its sad and unvarying record with the glory and brightness and final triumph of our country's civilization. With the garnered wealth of our land held firmly in our strong hands, guarded and controlled by the unimpaired spirit of our citizenship—instead of this material era, leaving us with an emasculated country with the true aims of government perverted—before our majestic progress mankind will, like Elijah at Horeb, wrap its face in its mantle before the glory of the works of God.

The exaltation of our civilization cannot be wrought to its final accomplishment, unless accompanied in the

life of the citizen by a virtue exalted beyond temptation and by a love of country dimmed by no desire
of acquisition. By virtue, I mean virtue in its highest
and most exalted sense, civic virtue. Build your empire of commerce on the sea; grasp in your hands all
the peoples of the earth; let your civilization and trade
and power be stretched from Southern Cross to Arc-
turus; enshrine the glories gathered on sea and land
in temples stately beyond the knowing of man; unless
all is builded on these highest human ideals, as sure as
man is born of woman, you have founded an empire
of unrest. Lighting the earth by the wonders of science
and touching the peoples with our triumphs of commerce will be small when weighed with the potency
of our example for good or for evil on the nations of
the earth. With no sense of national exultation, but
appreciating its responsibility, I assert that the character of the American citizen will determine the character of this age. Your eyes will behold three hundred
millions of people dwelling in this land, one-half of
civilized mankind, and the grandeur of their influence
will partake of the majesty of our country. We are
charged with the happiness of mankind. Is not this
responsibility above every question of personal consideration? Does it not reach to a higher element in our
life than the mere question of personal gain? "What
is the individual man with all the good or evil that
may betide him in comparison with the good or evil
which may befall a great country in a crisis like this,

and in the midst of great transactions which concern that country's fate?''

When in time was the virtue of citizenship so important to a country as it is to us in this era? When in the broad world did justice need sword so bright or lance so strong? When did the world call so loudly for a country exalted by the spirit of justice and filled with the supreme desire to maintain its principles? When nations, whose sceptered masters, are crowned by the servants of Him who gave to mankind the law of equity between peoples and men, measure justice alone by rule of diplomat and strength of serried battalions should not virtue have a champion with no thought but of justice? When the great nations, hoary with civilization, divide an empire under the pretence of commercial concessions, delimitate spheres of influence which violate the fundamental principles of human decency, and assume jurisdictions subversive of the laws of nations, surely justice is beating with impatient hands upon the temple door. When ships, swinging under the banners of civilization, are laden with looted treasure of temple and palace, it needs only change of time and place to bring before us the ox-wagons of Attila and Alaric, piled high with the household goods of Gaul and Rome. Verily,

> "The good old rule, the simple plan,
>   That they do take who have the power,
>   And they do keep who can."

Before scenes like these civilization bows her head

and with lifted hands prays for a force among the peoples of the world holding that justice and virtue between men and nations are builded on the same eternal foundations. Under the earth-hunger of to-day justice among the nations can only relume her torch from the shrine of virtue glowing in the heart of the great Republic of the West.

I implore that like the Vestal Virgins you will, with unceasing watchfulness, keep the flame pure and strong. Before the temptations of this colossal age the black page of civic infamy grows insignificant. The commercial combinations of the era, controlling every product of our country and overstepping all of the barriers of existing law, sternly demand that legislative control which will forever fix their correct position in our country's life. We must surround these creations of the era with that wise legislation and with those restrictions which a free people has learned through sad experience must always control the exercise of naked power. Dominated by the citizen, holding no power above laws and constitutions, they must take their place in our civic life and play their legitimate part in the affairs of this splendid era. This result can never be accomplished without a struggle unexampled in historic experience. Since man began to earn his bread by the sweat of his brow, power never loosened its heavy hand without a struggle, fierce and relentless though it may be. Did ever power plead for such a stake? Did ever greed hover over such fertile fields?

A judgment of court means wealth greater than the income of kings; a line of legislation is an imperial tribute; and the success of an election is the control of the world. When Bacon, the wisest of mankind, threw himself at the feet of the Commons and, with passionate cry, exclaimed, "I do plainly and ingenuously confess that I am guilty of corruption and do renounce all defence," his whole briberies on the bench of the highest court of the world did not amount to a day's income of a modern king of commerce. When Buckingham wasted the treasure of England, leaving to us John Eliot's invective, that precious heritage of freedom, "This only is conceived by us, knights, citizens, and burgesses of the Common House of Parliament, that by him came all our evils, in him we find the causes, and on him must be the remedies. *Pereat qui perdere cuncta festinat. Opprimatur ne omnes opprimat*," his whole profligate expenditure of the wealth of a great kingdom would not suffice for the yearly needs of an industrial corporation of this era. When Edmund Burke, " In the name of the people of India, whose rights he has trodden under foot and whose country he has turned into a desert," arraigned Warren Hastings, all the peculation charged against the founder of English Asiatic Empire, wrung from lordly India through years of uncontrolled power, would not tell the tale of the golden stream falling for one season into the vaults of an American temple of exchange.

Is it not, however, wasting of precious time for me

to consider that you will put aside the benediction of the republican honor and virtue coming to you as a priceless heritage of the past? The blood coursing through your veins, throbbing from the lives of two hundred years of honest men and women, will not allow you to be paid participants in unjust legislation or to utter the judgments of corrupted court. "Only continue to be what you are. Let your government commence in your breast; and lay the foundation of it in the command of your passions. If you make virtue the rule of your conduct, and the end of your actions, everything will proceed in harmony and order. I have explained to you the spirit of those laws and con-stitutions that were established by your predecessors; and you have nothing to do but to carry them into execution. If this should be the case, I shall have the glory of having formed an emperor to virtue; but if otherwise, let this letter remain a testimony with succeeding ages, that you did not ruin the Roman Empire under pretence of the counsels or the authority of Plutarch."

When Rome heard these words, as applicable to-day to our Republic as it was to Rome in the days of Trajan, it was too late. The rule of material power had usurped the place of patriotism in the breasts of the people, and the once mistress of the world had not the strength to resist the wave of barbaric invasion. It was but the reiteration of the eternal rule as to the violation of the underlying principles of the people.

Was ever a great and permanent monument erected by a historic people but its foundations were built broad and deep upon that perception and life which recognized that virtue and patriotism were the most exalted attributes of the citizen? Only founded upon these attributes, I repeat, can a people become permanent and hold its place against the changes wrought by time. To sell the cheapest wares, to sail the swiftest ships, to load the world with the best bargains, to erect the most magnificent mills and manufactories, are the smallest part of the work which a great and free people are destined to accomplish. These ideals have only left toppling ruins in the history of the peoples of the world. They have never accomplished great and abiding results. Within themselves and strengthened by all of the tremendous forces at their command, these ideals cannot impress our civilization upon the world. To successfully accomplish this and impress the noblest ideals and the highest aspirations upon the world, our country must fill its wealth of enterprise with the exalted patriotism of a free people. To arouse our country to these highest elements of citizenship is our supreme duty. To fill it with the noblest resolve should be our first thought. This is supreme to any question of material power and its selfish advantages. This spirit will fill our ships with more favorable breezes and strengthen our hands among the nations of the earth. It will do far more; it will place our country upon foundations high above the danger of governmental and commercial change. You cannot subordinate patriotism to acquisition, nor make the spirit of the day the chief object of our civil existence. This era must and surely will run its course, but our country must live for its high destiny. Exalted and strengthened with holy love of country, all of the questions of our governmental and civil life will be settled in their allotted time. Flushed with our success, confident in our strength, we only discern questions of unrest in the far distance. With the filling of our vacant lands, the changing of the relations of the citizens each to the other, the increase of cost of living, the settling of the conditions of class steadily approximating those conditions in the older countries of the world, the hardening of the struggle for existence among our people will surely bring questions to disturb and to annoy. With these potential dangers before us, I pray for that wealth of patriotism underflowing our material life which will create that mighty moral power that will enable our country to pass successfully this great cycle of change.

Edmund Burke says that it is the highest duty of a citizen to make the most of the materials of his country. Were ever such materials laid in the palm of his hand to mould as he may desire? A noble, free people, crowned with a civilization unexampled, peopling a majestic continent crowded with every element of human happiness—will you not be recreant to your traditions if, with these transcendent materials, you do not make the world holier and better, and advance your country beyond the doors of the world's market-places? In the shade of these mountains and touched with the glory of this historic valley, what other senti-ment could we feel than that exalted spirit which holds as small every feeling of material aggrandizement as compared with love of country?

It seems that the people of the mountains hold more jealously to the great primal faiths of our country. I know not why, but we of the mountains have a simpler faith and feel more deeply the im-pairment of these great principles than do the people of the plain. From these heights the vision is clearer, and it pierces the clouds whose shadows are over the rich plains and fertile valleys. In the history of freedom and religion, the mountains of the world have played a mighty part. They alone have looked upon the ineffable majesty of God. In the mountains Moses met God, and Nebo's stony sides trembled with the thunder of the stern command, " Get thee up into this mountain and die." Their silent fastnesses wit-nessed the agony of the temptation of our Lord. To the eyes of faith arise Hermon and Tabor and Car-mel and Gilead and the hills of Galilee echoing with the footsteps of Prophet and Patriarch and King and Disciple. When religious and political freedom had no abiding-place, the song of the Huguenot swelled pure and triumphant amid the mountains of France. When the light grew faint in the Mother Country, over the mountains of Scotland stood the pillar of cloud by day and of fire by night. When from the plains of Po to the German Ocean the weary feet of freedom had no resting-place, it fled to the cliffs of the Alps and found there a home.

When in our own country liberty had almost despaired of triumph, the Father of his Country turned his despairing eyes to these mountains, here to plant the banner of freedom and maintain among this liberty-loving people the contest for its existence. So to-night I would bid you to look above the glories of this material age and ascend the mountains on whose lofty sides dwells patriotism, whose life is infinitely more superior in importance to mankind than all of the teeming plenty in the plains beneath.

From these supreme heights sprung the men of Virginia whose lives are the loftiest contemplation for those who, during this momentous period, will control the destiny of our country. Surrounded by the majesty of nature, its influence broadened their every thought and elevated every principle of action. With the grandeur of mountain and tenderness of outline and color always before them, love of country was pre-eminent to all thought of self. *Cari sunt parentes, cari liberi, cari familiares, propinqui; sed omnes omnium caritates una patria complexa est*—"Sweet are parents, sweet are children, sweet are friends and relations; but all affections of all men are embraced in country alone" was not merely the swelling period of the philosopher and orator, but was to them the eternal truth whose verity they were full ready to prove by giving up all save country. From these exalted scenes rose the men, the like of whom the world has yet to see.

Partaking from their surroundings of that nobleness of spirit which loved truth because it was true and cared naught for wealth when weighed in the balance with love of country, ease and luxury and power were thrown aside without a sigh when country called them to its sacred sacrifice. This greatness of spirit, this contemplation of lofty ideals for themselves and country never lessened that effectiveness which in the world of thought, in the wide domain of government, and on the active theatre of life, wrought for mankind those mighty works whose life will march with time.

When the ancients wished to begin any important work, through the smoke of shrines lighted by anxious hands they summoned the gods from broad Olympus and wooded Ida. Here in the shadows of these mountains, mute but eternal witnesses of Virginia's toil and sacrifices, I would summon around you from the battle-field and council-chamber her mighty spirits whose holy influence may cause you to pluck from your hearts any love greater than that of country, to exalt with holy pride of patriotism your every aspiration and desire, and to so cherish your country's honor that from her stately portals she may walk among the nations with uplifted countenance and hands unsullied. Here, in old Virginia's land, I would surround you with spirits more glorious than any worshipped in marble fane on Thessalian mountain-top. Here would I assemble your fathers, proud spirits of freedom, and, uplifted by their unseen presence, pray that the civilization erected by them should never be sullied by wrong. Where, in what land, can you touch such holy inspiration for love of country, and if, holding for naught their sacrifices and tears, with impious hands you should touch this temple of the world's hopes, where so deep a curse? With every swelling mountain a temple of memories, holy and sweet, and every valley a tented field where wait in rest the spectred hosts of Virginia's glorious dead, touched with the grace of such example, you can do naught of dishonor to your country's life. Proud Virginia, matchless mother of stately sons, self-immolated on freedom's altar, with thy bosom seamed and torn, yet with thy soul white and pure, thy sons greet thee, and touching hands around thy altar, they swear fealty to truth and honor. And oh, my country, above thy stately palaces, higher than the splendors of thy labor born from thy heart of endeavor, may thou erect a temple, enduring and glorious, which will be crowned with a citizenship matchless in its intelligence, unapproachable in its virtue, whose light shall touch with gladness and hope all the nations which on this earth do dwell!

VI

PATRIOTISM OF THE SOUTH [1]

Mr. President, Ladies, and Gentlemen :

W HEN your honored invitation came it carried me in my thoughts to Virginia, to the Great Valley where I first saw the light. With the glamour of youth's enchantment lingering yet a little, I saw old Virginia's hills with the sunshine glorifying farm and village, mirroring itself in the bright waters, and clothing mountain and valley with wealth of green and gold. A vision came to me of the old Commonwealth as I remember it in my childhood. Again I saw her worn from battle-field and adversity, again I witnessed her sorrows, her sacrifices, her courage, her high honor, her glory, everything save dishonor.

This fair valley still reverberated with the thunderous tread of the angel of the spear and the sword. Never since Alaric harried Italy and Gaul, never since Alva ravaged the Low Countries has the hand of fate held for a people such hard conditions.

I wish to awaken no sad memories, for your faces are turned to the glory of the rising morning, not to the rays of the setting sun. Yet, in the pages of what

[1] An address delivered June 17, 1908, before the Literary Societies of Washington and Lee University, Lexington, Va.

book, from the broad field of what experience, can I
better gather for you lessons of high resolve than from
the heroic endeavor and exalted ideals with which our
fathers and mothers crowned with unexampled grace
this land of the South?

Here in this old State, my native land, under the
portal of this hoary University, listening to the heart-
throbs of those whose blood flows with mine, feeling
the touch of unseen hands, and hearing the music of a
voice tuned to the choir of the Blessed, I am surrounded
by the tender memories of the days that are gone. An
angel winged its way to our earth to find here the
sweetest and best to take back to the radiance of
Heaven. There was wafted on the sunshine the perfume of the rose and it was garnered as worthy to enter
the holy streets. Anon, under the shadows of the
gathering evening, the smile of a babe as it slept in its
cradle was clasped to the bosom of the messenger, and
then, beneath the drooping eaves of an humble cottage,
there was found a mother's love. When at the Pearly
Gates the bosom of the angel was loosed of its burden,
the perfume of the rose had wasted, the smile of the
babe had waned, and the mother's love alone was left
to pass the lintel of Heaven.

God bless my mother's love. Everything that I am
is her honor and here at her old home, glorified with
her love and ennobled by her sacrifices, I wish in this
splendid presence to make to her memory my loving
obeisance. God bless our mothers of our South, from

whose spotless souls came our earliest aspirations for good, who, when the cruse of oil was failing and the meal in the barrel was wasting, looked with eyes of hope beyond that of men, to that better land where the dews are distilled into plenty and where the prayers of faith are always answered!

God bless the mothers of the South! When our fair land was wasted and war had ploughed deep and broad the furrow which divided the affections of our country, it was the mother who, walking firmly and securely with Him who said, "And unto him that smiteth thee on the one cheek, offer also the other," taught the sections those exalted humanities which bound again in love and confidence the peoples of this great nation.

With splendid resolve the men and women of the South turned their lives to the broken home and the desolate field, to the rebuilding of our prostrate civilization, and the song of the wheels is not their requiem but a pæan of victory.

These fields of plenty about us, this glory of completed endeavor, this marvellous re-creation and perpetuation of the life of the South attest to us the exalted patriotism of our fathers, which is of infinite importance to the country in the changes of the day. It is this patriotism of the South, and its influences upon the present, which in my homely manner I wish to present in this discourse.

From the very texture of its civilization, the origin

and habits of its people, and their political and social as well as local environment, the South has been beyond other people with whom I am acquainted controlled by ideals. The controlling ideal of the South has been patriotism, the patriotism of State and locality.

I do not apologize for the theme. It is old fashioned, but amidst the complication of the affairs of modern life, and considering the change of the texture of thought as to governmental direction, is it not best for us to recur to those fundamental ideals which controlled in the formation of our country's government?

Under the conditions of the day the patriotism of the South along its conservative lines as to governmental direction should have the amplest and fullest play. As the country grows in power it grows naturally along the lines of organization and concentration. That organization is directed largely to results. Those results, under the general ideals of the day, are peculiarly economic. The consequence is that the man becomes a mere unit in the sum-total of production. He looks at the marvellous results, and, in a way, is proud of his country, yet he is endangered of becoming lessened in his dignity, his aspirations, and his patriotism. The patriotism which I mean is not that which counts the glory of our country solely by the ships on the sea, the glowing furnaces, and the fertile acres, but the patriotism which cherishes and loves this wonderful combination of State and Union, and ennobles and glorifies the aspirations of the citizen.

As in economic life, such is the trend of the governmental conditions of the day. This great Union has dazzled the world by its accomplishment. It has waged successful wars on land and sea. It has covered the sea with ships and commerce. It has accomplished wonders of diplomacy among the peoples of the earth. By its laws it has dimmed the stars with the smoke of its manufactories. It is binding together the oceans and mingling the waters of the lakes. It has built harbors and deepened rivers. It has constructed a great system of judiciary. Through its Congress it has thrown the robe of its power over the whole people, and has touched with its strong hands every work and aspiration and sentiment. It has accomplished marvels, but, in that accomplishment, there is with many, especially of the South, an abiding fear that this has been wrought to the lessening of the influence and powers of the State under the Constitution. The most precious thing which we who are older can give to the young is experience. This experience teaches me the trend of the day and that it should be the supreme object of patriotism to guide the government into the old channels provided by the Fathers.

Thoughtful men believe that in the South abides that ideal of local patriotism which can accomplish this mighty work, and preserve unimpaired this marvellous combination of State and Union.

Can this Southern patriotism be successfully appealed to under the conditions of the present? Is it alive and virile? Are the basic ideas of the South yet sufficiently strong to influence the direction of the whole people? Is the material power of the South of sufficient potency to dignify its demand for the return to these basic principles? To answer these questions we must understand the history and underlying principles of our Southern people.

It is interesting to observe that the vital characteristic of Southern patriotism had its written origin in a charter granted by a Stuart. The General Assembly which met for the first time in America had well defined rights as to local liberty. It is true its acts must be affirmed by the General Court, but in the Charter there was the great, vital, salient germ of constitutional government that no Orders of Court could be enforced without the approval and affirmance of the General Assembly. These principles of this Charter did not spring from the ground. Its great principle of local, representative government was not born fully developed from the head of the goddess. It was not evolved from the limpid waves, the smiling sun, the giant trees, and the fertile soil of Virginia. The old chroniclers say that the Charter was granted upon the insistent demands of the Virginians. The Virginians consisted at that time of not more than two thousand people, but even in this handful, in a new country and beside the waters of strange seas, the spirit of local liberty was rife, and they had brought with them the desire that the rights for which they were contending

in old England should be granted them in this
country.

The times were propitious for the growth of civil
liberty, and surely patriotism should twine itself about
the fair lands into which these strangers had come.
The forcing of the written Charter of 1621 for local
liberty by Sir Edwin Sandys and his compatriots, in
England, confirming by general grant the Assembly's
acts of 1619, was but the evidence in Virginia of the
great contest in their native England. England was
changing. Henry and Elizabeth, with the glamour
which power and personal beauty and strength of
character always engender in the people, were asleep
in Westminster Abbey. A tyrannical bigot not respected for strength or character and hated for his
course against the liberty of the people was in their
place. The England which confronted Elizabeth in
the days of her power was even more insistent upon its
rights. The supremacy of Parliament, freedom of conscience, liberty of the judges, exclusive right of taxation and absolute control of the revenues by Parliament,
and representation by the people, were the watchwords
of the England which witnessed the dawning of governmental life in America.

" That the liberties, franchises, privileges, and jurisdictions of Parliament are the ancient and undoubted
birthright and inheritance of the subjects of England;
and that the arduous and urgent affairs concerning
the King, State, and defence of the Realm, and of the

Church of England, and the making and maintenance of laws, and redress of grievances, which daily happen within this Realm, are proper subjects and matter of Council and debate in Parliament. And that in the handling and proceeding of those businesses every member of the House hath, and of right ought to have, freedom of speech to propound, treat, reason, and bring to conclusion the same," was the demand of the Commons.

Silhouetted upon the canvas were the dread figures of Pym, and Elliott, and Hampden, and England was listening even then for the heavy step of Oliver Cromwell.

It was England of the Remonstrance, of the Petition of Right, of the Revolution, of the Supremacy of Parliament ; and Scotland of the Covenant, and France of the Reformation, which furnished the swaddling clothes for our constitutional liberty.

Patriotism does not mean the mere love of the concrete portion, the mountains, the rivers, and the fertile lands, of a country. It means far more than this. It means love of country, crowned with pure and free and good government, liberty of conscience and religion, justice, government by those who bear the government's burdens, and the high ideals reverenced by the people.

Patriotism supposes a country and traditions, and the struggle of years for the great principles demanded by the life of the people. It was seven hundred years after the foundation of Rome before patriotism prompted the Grachii to revolt. It was a thousand years of English conflict before love of England forced the people to a war with the king, in which conflict the control of the government was the wager of battle. It was an equal stretch of weary struggle before the white banner of Joan of Arc was unfurled in France. So it has been heretofore with every historic country which has witnessed the evolution and completion of the ideals of patriotism.

In our land the struggle for the attainment of these high ideals lasted only a short time. Here in five generations of men was the accomplishment of the ideals of patriotism in this their loftiest meaning. We again insist that the patriotism which has crowned this marvellous work in our country did not have its birth on these shores. It was in the struggling for life at Runnymede. It was in the Scotch Revolution. It was in the Utopia of Sir John Moore. It was with Wycliff, John Ball, Knox, and John Calvin. The patriotism of which I speak was being born in the breasts of the peoples who formed the South. Consider these peoples. They are bone of your bone and blood of your blood. The glory of a country is the perpetuation of the great characteristics of its citizens. The people from whom you sprung have been peculiar in the perpetuation and procreation of the principles which made them great. Here in the South there has been little admixture of foreign blood. In almost every case you are the sons of those who were at Valley Forge, King's Mountain, Cowpens, and Yorktown. That the characteristics of the fathers ring clear in their children is the prayer of those who love their country.

Let us consider for a moment the texture of the life and the salient principles of those who largely controlled and composed Southern life, and, who, in a great degree, directed in the formative period. They have been cruelly neglected in the written history and the spoken word of our common country.

What was the moving cause of their coming to this land? Excepting the Latins in Louisiana and Florida and the early adventurers, migration to this land is but an index to governmental crime in Europe against local right, religious and personal freedom. With relatively few exceptions it was the expatriation of people who above everything loved freedom of thought and conscience, and governmental justice. It was the expatriation of people worn with ceaseless struggle for principle and whose hands were red with blood shed for the right to live under the laws of their country according to the dictates of their conscience. The decks of every ship whose sails were swelled with the western breeze were filled with those who looked back upon the receding shores of their native land, whose hills were crowned with the altars erected for the immolation of the ideals which they loved, and whose valleys were filled with their trampled fields and ruined homes.

Theretofore in all the history of time there had never been an expatriation of a people solely for the high ideals of life. Here in the South is the building of a people whose fundamental elements are composed, be they French, English, or Scotch, of peoples who loved these lofty ideals, rather than life or worldly possessions, and who always stood ready to give life and possessions for those ideals. However diverse these may have been, whether reverencing, as the loftiest ideal, church and state with the Cavalier, or toleration with the Scotchman and the Huguenot, or clinging to local self-government with the Englishman, yet all were patriotic idealists. In every other instance since the pages of history were opened, the betterment of the material condition has been the sole and underlying cause of the movement of a people.

The great Aryan change was at the command of an instinct for more fertile fields and wider lands. The Hebrew movement was under the commands of the Almighty, guided by the cloud and fiery pillar. The Greek migrated into Greater Greece that he might build city, and gymnasium, and temple, and cultivate fertile fields denied to him by the narrow confines of his own land. The Roman went into Africa, Spain, Greece, Gaul, and Germany that the Roman colonist might hold with his strong hands the lands conquered with the sword. The Goth and Visi-Goth immigration was for pure lust of conquest. The Mohammedan moved under the influence of a religion dictated by the physical betterment of its adherents, both in this life and in the life to come. The invasion by the Norman of England was, alone and solely, for power and territory. The immigration of the Frenchman and the Englishman into Canada and of the English in the East and the Antipodes, and the movement of the Spaniard into South America and the Islands of the Seas, were for gold, jewels, land, and dominion, and nothing more.

In none of these great movements was there a seeking alone for the higher ideals of government or life, nor was there in any case holier influence than the desire of betterment of material well-being. Entirely different were the motives of those creating the South.

The Cavalier under his plumed bonnet and curled locks carried a love of Church and King unquenchable, and placed above castle and ancestral manor undying loyalty to his ideal of his country governed by the system bequeathed to him from his fathers. Amidst the blazing rafters and the falling walls of his house he could exclaim with the old Marquis of Winchester, "That if the King had no more ground in England than Basing House, he would adventure it as he did, that Basing House was called Loyalty," or answer with Sir Henry Washington, when asked to surrender Worcester, "That he would await the commands of the King." Not until Naseby, Worcester, Marston Moor, Newbury, and Dunbar had shown that their cause was dead on the field of battle and that the principles they revered were trampled under the feet of

Cromwell and the Ironsides, did these people give back their hands and knees one inch. Only when the struggle was lost at home, the white sails of their ships brought them to the South, where, under the glory of our Southern sun and the influence of life under our institutions, loyalty to the ideal of England under King and Church was reincarnated into the higher and holier love of a country which prescribes no religion and exacts no toll from conscience.

One more persistent, more earnest, and who exerted a greater influence upon Southern life in the actual struggle for liberty than the Cavalier, was the Scotch Covenanter, the Scotch-Irishman of this day and place.

Proscribed by law, massacred on heathery mountain, starved on frozen moor, yet above massacre of wife and children, proscription of law, and through the smoke of burning home and amidst the desolation of field and country, he clung to the religious ideal of the Covenant:

"We promise and swear, by the great name of the Lord, our God, to continue in the profession and obedience of the said religion; and that we shall defend the same, and resist all their contrary errors and corruptions, according to our vocation and to the utmost of that power which God has put in our hands, all the days of our life."

A people of whom Mr. Bancroft has said: "The first voice publicly raised in America to dissolve all connection with Great Britain came not from the

Puritans of New England, nor the Dutch of New York, nor the planters of Virginia, but from the Scotch-Irish Presbyterians,"—the glory of whose character reaches its culmination in the words of the Covenanter John Witherspoon before the Continental Congress :

"To hesitate at this moment is to consent to our slavery. That noble instrument upon your table . . . should be subscribed this very moment by every pen in this house. He that will not respond to its accents, and strain every nerve to carry into effect its provisions, is unworthy the name of freeman, . . . and although these gray hairs must descend into the sepulchre, I would infinitely rather that they should descend hither by the hand of the executioner than desert at this crisis the sacred cause of my country."

In this Southern land mingled with Covenanter and Cavalier and Puritan the blood of the Huguenot who for his ideal for more that two centuries in France, from the Rhine to the Mediterranean, marked the faggot and the gibbet, and could match Claverhouse with the Guise, Derry with La Rochelle, and the wild moors of Scotland and wasted fields of Antrim with the desolate mountains of Cevennes.

And I make my obeisance to the German, the Irishman, and the Puritan of the South, than whom lived no purer patriots, but I am speaking of the controlling strains in the South.

Those peoples largely composing the Southern people were dominated by high and peculiar ideals of local, governmental, and religious right. Yet, whilst they loved their country, they were controlled and largely limited in their aspirations by the ideal for which they contended. In almost every case in their own country they would have been satisfied with the attainment of that ideal. The Scot was contending with his whole soul for religious toleration, the Cavalier for his ideal of Church and King, and the Frenchman for a condition which would free him from social, religious, and governmental tyranny of king and noble. With the controlling ideal of the Scotchman, the Cavalier, and the Englishman, there was the almost equally abiding ideal of local control. They all loved their country, but in a secondary or subconscious manner. They were developing patriotism. Each of these peoples was grasping, at different times, and in diverse ways, all of its vital elements ; and, whilst contending for the high ideals which they loved, they were contending for the highest and best constituents of patriotism. In every case this ideal, whether it might be religious toleration and freedom, or equal taxation and representation, or freedom from class and governmental injustice, exalted the country and increased immeasurably the moral stature of the citizen. Yet these constituents did not culminate there in the great, vital, and absorbing ideal of patriotism.

How quickly do we note this differentiation between the people from whom we sprung whilst living in their own country, and, afterwards, when living in this country. There, loyalty to a family, a king, a system of religion, was the highest ideal of life. Here, under our skies, not environed by the trappings of monarchy and traditions of caste and system, and appreciating through fierce experiences that his efforts alone were to conquer and control the new land, the American colonist quickly and powerfully grasped the great proposition that he was the supreme figure and that the country and its government belonged to him, and to him alone. Here, he was dealing directly with his country, of which he knew he was the most important constituent. There, he had grown with the generations who believed the government could not be conducted without the king and the system surrounding him. As a matter of fact, in the beginning, when the king was filled with prowess and character, this was largely the truth. He was the king because he was necessary to the conditions of the time. Here, the colonist soon recognized a changed condition, that in clearing the forest, defending his home, and creating government, kingly leadership and trappings were useless and that he was the state and practically the responsible head of the government.

Thus, no king or system could be the supreme object of his affection and nothing intervened between him and love of the state, which, without help of king, noble, or class, he was creating. When surveying the vast forest, the majestic rivers, the unploughed land, and the smiling valleys, he recognized that he was the central figure of this marvellous panorama. Thus, amidst

the majesty and, so far as the government was concerned, the isolation of his surroundings, there arose in
his heart a feeling towards his country differing entirely
from the sentiment that at home environed the Englishman, the Frenchman, or Scotchman.

In other words, there was born pure and undefiled
patriotism, love of country, with the intervention of no
lesser ideal which could diminish the splendor of its
aspiration.

When you consider the limitations surrounding those
who largely composed the Southern colonists, nothing
in history is so eloquent as the growth of this spirit of
patriotism in the South. At the first, especially in
Virginia, which we have taken as a type, its inhabitants
were largely Cavaliers environed by the supreme ideal
of loyalty to the king. They had been practically ex-
patriated for this ideal; yet, under and around this
loyalty to the king, there was growing the great and
supreme principle of love of our country for itself, with
the control of the government by the people as the
living, breathing essence and evidence of that patriotism. How marvellous was its development under these
adverse circumstances. A sentiment which for one
moment of time, strengthened immeasurably by the
arrival of those oppressed in Scotland, Ireland, and
England, never ceased its steady step. Contemplate
the milestones on the road to this ideal. The path was
tortuous, weary with waiting, and rank with the weeds
and grasses of wrongs which could not be resented; yet

along its whole length on ever broadening foundations are the monuments of our fathers' patriotism.

Pardon the taking of precious time in this phase of the discussion, but what can be more eloquent, what more interesting than the contemplation of the growth of love of one's country? Patriotism in every country is distinct and moves along distinct lines. Here in the South was the growth of patriotism along the distinct lines of local self-government, which ever widened in its scope. Before the ink was dry on the Charter of 1619, the Assembly of Virginia, catching with its first lisping the breath of freedom, demanded that the Company might "allow or disallow of their Orders of Court, as his Majesty hath given them power to allow or disallow our laws." Here was asserted in full life the great and underlying principle of our governmental existence. Within five years came the memorable declaration of 1624, "that the governor shall not lay any taxes or impositions upon the colony, their lands or commodities, otherway than by the authority of the General Assembly, to be levied and employed as the said Assembly shall appoint."

Men who were felling forests, ploughing the unfurrowed land, and subduing a mighty wilderness in 1635, thrust out Governor Harvey and elected a successor, because he would not forward their protest to his Majesty. By 1650 the Englishman was a Virginian, the Cavalier a patriot, and above loyalty to the king there had been developed the supreme ideal of love of country. When the Commissioners of Cromwell came to take over the government of Cavalier Virginia, they did not find the colonists with diverse ideas of loyalty, a population distraught with divergent sentiments of fealty, but they found a people with one growing supreme ideal and that was love of their country, with the right to control their own local affairs, and this ideal was superior to fealty to king or English Commonwealth. The conference was between two powers each filled with its distinctive idea, and Virginia forced from the victors of Naseby and Dunbar the concession that she was "to enjoy such freedoms and privileges as belong to the free-born people of England"; and the Virginia Assembly was alone to have the right to tax Virginia. Yet, within ten years, with the downfall of the government of Cromwell, and the re-induction into power of the king, Cavalier Virginia, caring first for Virginia and little for its old ideal, forced from Governor Berkeley, the representative of the fealty of the Cavalier, that he was to govern according to the laws of Virginia and England, that he was not to dissolve the Assembly without the consent of a majority of its members, and every writ was to run in the name of the Assembly of Virginia.

Growing patriotism was demanding first the rights of the colony, and, as a secondary consideration, fealty to king.

A century before the Revolution how ominous to king and to England is the ring of the words of

Nathaniel Bacon, a son of an English gentleman, who then held arms in his hand for love of the new country:

"That it is the mind of this country, and of Mary Land and Carolina also, to cast off their Governor, and the Governors of Carolina have taken no notice of the People, nor the People of them, a long time; and the people are resol'd to own their Governour further; And if wee cannot prevaile by Armes to make our Conditions for Peace, or obtaine the Priviledge to elect our own Governour, we may retire to Roanoke."

The old ideal of fealty to king and family and system was falling like the forest and in its stead was growing that ideal of patriotism which I pray and trust is glorifying the opening of your young lives.

This spirit did not grow in the souls of men whose lives were given to contemplation of government. There were other things to consider and to accomplish. It was accompanied by the twang of the bow, the flash of the musket, the burning of the home, and with the waving corn trampled in ground wet with the blood of savage conflict. It grew with the ring of the axe, the birth of the children, with the furrow of the plough, with the founding of towns and cities, with the creation of states, with institution of laws, with starvation and fever, with wrong in England, and oftentimes with bigotry and narrowness at home.

It assumed many shapes, but in every case and contest, through every difficulty and complication, there was the one supreme and controlling idea which had for its purpose the right of the new country and control of its affairs.

When the right of the colony was concerned, Cavalier, Roundhead, Scotch-Irishman, or Frenchman was ready, irrespective of former fealty or connection, to contest with king or Commonwealth. Patriotism was grasping firmly the soul of the people. In one colony and period it took the form of opposition to the Navigation Act and in another to have free intercourse with other colonies. Again it blazed forth over the question of the method of appointing the parsons. Here, reasoning from the experience of their fathers in England, they withheld supplies until grievances were righted. There, it was as to basis of representation. Then it showed its life in unceasing opposition to the prerogatives of the governor appointed by the king. In Virginia, whilst the postage laws were obviously beneficial and important, the Virginians would not allow the enforcing of the act, because they believed that Parliament had in its passage interfered with the authority of the House of Burgesses in regard to local government.

"No sooner was this noised about but a great Clamour was raised against it. The people were made to believe that the Parl't could not Levy and Tax (for so they call ye Rates of Postage) here without the Consent of the General Assembly. . . . Thereupon a Bill is prepared and passed both Council and Burg's's, w'ch, tho' it acknowledges the Act of Parliam't to be in force here, does effectually prevent its being ever put in Execution,'' was the complaint of Governor Spottswood.

With all the tenacity attending the conflict from Magna Charta down to the end of the Stuart Tyranny, the colonists never lessened their grim determination to absolutely control taxation, and never once was relinquished their effort both to pass every act concerning taxation and to expend the money derived therefrom.

This ideal of patriotism, with its years of sorrow, of travail, and of creation, culminated in the resolutions of Patrick Henry in the Virginia House of Burgesses, in the Declaration of 1776, and the Convention of 1788.

It seemed wise that there should be a dual system of government and before the wasted field was clothed in its robe of green, and ere the patriot had begun to realize his freedom, the divergence began as to the unit of the ideal of the patriotism which is so vitally important to a free government.

Let me here be clearly understood that in choosing as the subject of this address the patriotism of the South, it is not to evince any sectional spirit. It is not from any want of catholic feeling. Whilst we of the South love our land with a wealth of tender sentiment, which possibly does not exist so markedly between other sections of our country and their citizens, because we and ours have sat with the South at the empty table and have walked with her along the road of sorrow, yet the supreme object of our patriotic love is this great Republic. No section can compare with the whole in our love and regard. Our country, undivided and indivisible, is a supreme object of our patriotic solicitude. Therefore, I am addressing myself to the peculiar spirit and local characteristics of the people of the South, which I believe can, and will, change the tendencies which are dangerous to the Republic.

At first in our country the unit of patriotism was the State. This was natural. This feeling was peculiarly strong in the South. It came about from the traditions of the people and the nature of their situation. The Southern colonies were far separated one from the other. Furthermore, from the difference in the character of charter or government each carried on its own contest for its local rights with the mother country or with the Indians who surrounded them. Each of the colonies was practically a republic. Their citizens met only infrequently, and there obtained the patriarchal and agricultural system which of itself maintained pristine sentiments and conditions.

The practical unit of livelihood was the isolated plantation, and thus each colony of the South had grown with a feeling of local independence. For protection or development it depended upon itself. Thus each colony gradually became individualistic in its sentiments, and was practically independent of the other colonies. Around its own government and its own affairs centred its affections. Agriculture and, latterly the production of two staples largely occupied the people's time and attention. The populations of the colonies of the South were largely homogeneous, and after the great Scotch-Irish immigration and the German immigration there was practically no immigration into the South. Men from the South who fought in the War of 1812 and the Mexican War and the War of 1860 were the sons and grandsons of the men who carried arms in the Revolution of 1776. The people of the South as I have endeavored to show sprang from the European peoples who had been from time immemorial contesting for their local rights.

Now, such was not the condition in the North. There the rigors of the climate and the topography of the country rapidly brought about a different situation. The people grew together in villages, the meetings between the colonies were relatively frequent. Their intercourse was comparatively easy. They did not preserve the homogeneity of their peoples. New peoples were continually arriving with new ideals, with diverse feelings, with no knowledge or care for the olden traditions of the State. Manufacturing occupied a country filled with rivers and waterfalls and they quickly turned to the sea and covered the ocean with their fleets.

At the time of the Declaration of Independence the ideal of local patriotism was earnest in the North as in the South. Massachusetts was at first filled with the local ideal, but the State was divided and her daughters necessarily did not preserve that ideal which had such vigorous life in the mother State. The diverse populations and interests of New York prevented the complete development of the local ideal of patriotism.

Notwithstanding these conditions, at first, in the North, fealty to the State obtained and this status largely controlled its sentiment for forty years after the Declaration of Independence. The unit of patriotism was local. Gradually, with the conditions I have mentioned, it began to change and the object of fealty began to be the General Government. Nationalization began to crystallize. New populations were occupying the towns and cities which were springing up in its manufacturing regions. When the new people came, in many instances they occupied new States which were the creations of the General Government. This feeling towards the National Government, this change of the unit of patriotism was increased and accentuated by the second War of Independence. It was enormously strengthened by the Mexican War. It was further strengthened by the economic condition of the North, whose manufacturing energies were largely benefited by the laws passed by the General Government.

The ideal of local patriotism in the North was changing into the ideal of personal liberty. Now do not understand me that there was any lessening of the patriotism of the North. Its ideal was simply changing with the times and with its natural conditions. As the ideal of patriotism generalized under the conditions of the day there quickly grew the ideal of personal liberty. This ideal was aided in its growth by the economic condition of the South. There the institution of slavery was the most marked development of the Southern life. It was lawful and was recognized by both North and South. Economically it was not suited to the North and soon free labor occupied its place.

With the growth of time there arose a sentiment which, so far as the North was concerned, partook of the moral ideal and, rapidly joining with the various causes which I have mentioned, begat in the North a different unit of patriotism. The North was gradually nationalizing around an issue which in its eyes had begun to be a moral issue. The South adhered to her old ideal of fealty to the State, of local patriotism, and being in close contact with those States which she conceived were interfering with her local rights and local institutions naturally intensified her feeling of patriotism to the State. The local unit of patriotism grew stronger with her. In other words, the South practically nationalized around the State, which was her pristine unit of patriotism. The North with her strengthened ideal of personal liberty and fealty to the General Government, which had gradually grown since 1825, believed that the South was violating the spirit of the Constitution, which guaranteed liberty to every man. The South, preserving her old ideals of local patriotism and State fealty, believed that with her was the great moral issue and that her ancient rights, securely preserved to her upon her entry into the General Government, were being infringed.

Hence arose the great moral conflict which settled the question of the constitutional secession of a State, but which left in the hearts of the Southern people that pristine ideal of local patriotism, which, while entirely loyal to the common country, believes that the great retained rights of the State under the Constitution of our fathers should ever remain unshorn of their power and unimpaired in their strength.

Is the South correct in its assertion that the preservation at this time of the full powers of the State under the Constitution is the exercise of the most exalted patriotism? Whilst we garnish and strengthen the great temple enshrining the General Government, shall we allow its stately proportions to obscure the lights burning upon the altars of the States? This is the great and insistent question. The Fathers considered the rights of the State as vital, that the General Government could not live without their absolute preservation, and that the essence of the government created by them was the preservation in its entirety of both divisions of our government. Is not this to-day as important as when our fathers entered upon the conflict for liberty? After all, it is supremely a question of liberty and its perpetnation. Liberty is the crowning glory of patriotism. Is it not as sweet to-day as it was to the Fathers? And should it not be as carefully nurtured? Shall we forget its importance in its continual use?

The Fathers had seen the splendor of the countries of history go down to darkness, and all from the same cause. They believed that in the system of representative government with local balances against the central power they had found the secret of free government which would go on forever. Upon this foundation they constructed a government which conserves, as never before, justice and liberty. Are not the mighty spirits of the Fathers yet with us and is not the perpetuation of these ideals of government the exercise of the most exalted patriotism?

"I will wait with hopes that the spirit which predominated in the Revolution is not gone, nor the cause of those attached to the Revolution lost."

That the supreme importance of the State may be recalled, and that you may realize that the Fathers believed that only through its preservation could this government be perpetuated, let us listen again to their words.

Says Patrick Henry in the Convention of 1788:

"States are the characteristics and the soul of a confederation. If the States be not the agents of this compact, it must be one great, consolidated, national government of the people of all the States."

Says Alexander Hamilton, himself no friend to great power in the State, yet recognizing that without it the General Government could not live:

"While the constitution continues to be read and its principles known, the states must, by every rational man, be considered as essential component parts of the union. . . . The destruction of the states must be at once a political suicide. Can the national government be guilty of this madness?''

And again :

'' It may safely be received as an axiom in our political system, that the state governments will, in all possible contingencies, afford complete security against invasions of the public liberty by national authority. In a confederacy, the people, without exaggeration, may be said to be entirely masters of their own fate.''

Listen to Edmund Pendleton :

'' It is the interest of the federal to preserve the state governments. . . . Unless there be state legislatures to continue the existence of congress, and preserve order and peace among the inhabitants, this general government, which gentlemen suppose will annihilate the state government, must itself be destroyed.''

Says Fisher Ames:

'' The state governments represent the wishes, and feelings, and local interests of the people. They will afford a shelter against the abuse of power; and will be the natural avengers of our violated rights.''

Said Oliver Ellsworth:

'' I turn my eyes to the states for the preservation of my rights. . . . The greatest happiness I expect in this life, I can derive from these alone. This happiness depends on their existence, as much as a new-born infant on its mother for nourishment."

Says Thomas Jefferson :

" The support of the State governments in all their rights, as the most competent administrations for our domestic concerns and the surest bulwarks against anti-republican tendencies."

Have not these words of the Fathers been verified by the accomplishment of nearly a century and a half of life? Where is there such freedom? What country has been blessed with such permanence and happiness and individual aspiration and liberty? Is not a theory of government so wonderful in its perpetuation along the lines laid out by them worthy to be adhered to in the strict letter of the Constitution? The Fathers had seen the robe of consolidated power cover whole peoples with its glitter and imperial grandeur. They had seen the liberty of many peoples go as surely as history writes its decrees.

Hence, not regarding their experience of contemporary government and the teachings of history, they adopted a system differing from all other governments. A system whose foundation is the State with vital inherent rights, including that of self-government, and a National Government of strictly enumerated powers under a rigid written constitution, with a disinterested tribunal to arbitrate the great questions arising under its dual system. Other times and countries had witnessed nationalized and imperial governments, but the distinguishing features of our government from others, as the Fathers created and intended it should live, is the life and structure of the individual State and the representation in the General Government based upon the State. Could a consolidated system have preserved our freedom and performed the important work demanded by the conditions of this Republic? Let us consider for a moment this most important question. Under the life of the State has grown an individuality, a local character, a personal liberty which could not grow under a consolidated government. Men at home have been creating States, developing State life and theories of State government, stamping individuality upon themselves, upon legislation, and upon the State, which could not occur under a centralized government. Men of the plough and the forest and the shop have been doing work which under other systems has been reserved for kings, and princes, and the great of the land.

The State has been the forum of the people. Upon it they have tried their experiments of law and legislation. Upon the State they have lavished their energy and their character. A vast country extending from ocean to ocean with diverse ideas and demands could only be developed by the marvellous workings of the state governments, each acting in its own way under control of its own citizens as its diverse situation and conditions demanded.

What a momentous part the State has played in that most important of all functions of free government, the creation of the citizen. What other system could be devised so well for this supreme purpose? He is part of the State, he sees the effect and tries the working of different theories of government upon the State whose rights are inherent and whose life touches the dignity and daily being of the people. The laws which he is creating are upon foundations free from assault by the majority in the General Government. This appeals to his local state pride. He contemplates the State in its evolution, and its character is the character which he himself imparts to it. Its dignity grows with his growth and its financial and governmental as well as moral integrity is the reflection of those exalted sentiments in his own bosom.

The State educates the citizen in a continuous civil existence, and only by this system could the control of its life be entirely under the supervision of the citizen.

The dual system as the Fathers created it has been the best method for the upbuilding of a new country. The citizen appreciates the peculiar needs of his State and from his experience its peculiar necessities are provided. Thus the local needs and sentiments of a State are conserved, both to become part of that abiding patriotism which grows with the citizen's pride in the creation of his own exertions and mind. By the self-denial and energy and honesty of the citizen arises the State, and hence grows in its heart that civic pride in its exalted characteristics which could not be felt towards a far-distant government, reaching down to an unmarked district or department.

Under the government of the State there has grown the most perfect system of domestic and local laws which has blessed the world. They are the laws which deserve the whole aspirations of the citizen's life and the holiest effort of his hands. These laws conserve every interest in his life. They are not laws created in a far-away capital of a consolidated country. They are the laws growing up under the supervision and control of the citizen himself. They are the laws which regulate the expenditures and control the sources of the supply. Under this system the citizen is not alone learning the great problems of State and self government, but whilst he is doing so he is assisting in the adorning and glorifying of the State in its material and civil life.

Where since work was given as the lot of man was there such field as the State for supreme efforts of an enlightened and interested patriotism? The laws of the State touch with living power every phase of existence. Her laws are the sacred laws. They are the laws upon which are founded the hearthstone. They are the home laws. They are the laws touching personal happiness, and to increase and conserve that happiness is the ultimate object of the State. They control taxation and through its power your land may glow with the yellow of the waving corn and with the miracle of the ripening fruit, or weep with the desolation and ruin wrought by the heavy step of the demagogue. They wave their mighty wand and school and college arise and carry blessed life-giving hope and aspiration into the souls of those who will adorn and glorify our citizenship. They directly reach the life of the banker with his dollars, the fisherman with his nets, the merchant with his wares, and the farmer with his lands. By their wisdom the wilderness sings with the music of the wheels and the mountain gives forth its riches reserved in its secret fastnesses by the Creator for the fruition of this thrice-blessed people. They hold justice with an even hand for rich and poor and pen the decrees of life and liberty. They punish the criminal, control disorder, and reward virtue. They surround your life in its every phase—then should they not have your patriotic effort ? Should not your love, your sacrifice, your honor, and your patriotism permeate the laws of the State as in the olden days the myrrh and frankincense filled the glory of the Temple? Surely the State has fulfilled the part designed for it by the Fathers, and is not this marvellous civilization a witness beyond compare against the sentiment which would impair the system which has wrought this wondrous result ?

With the States preserved in their inherent life under the dual system, the Fathers believed they had forever saved their country from the fears of despotism and the exercise of arbitrary power. It was not their intention to create a government where a great central power could be paramount. They preserved the States in all of their rights, except those rights which were expressly given to the General Government under the Constitution, and those rights so given were carefully guarded. They feared despotism and they loved liberty. With the rights of the States preserved, with the powers of the General Government delimited and rigidly defined, the central power could not obtain undue power.

How carefully are the rights of the States protected and their inherent powers preserved. How plainly is the belief of the Fathers shown, that liberty can only be perpetuated by a strict observance of the principles enumerated in the Constitution and the amendments thereto. It is but evident that they believed that these principles should control the future life of the country they were giving to their children. All of the great principles of liberty are carefully set out in the amendments to the Constitution, and every one of the original amendments is for the purpose of preserving in their entirety the reserved rights of the State and the liberties of the people. With the Constitution of our fathers casting around us its beneficent provisions, if we sacredly guard the exalted ideals of a patriotic people, if we preserve the rights secured to us by this wonderful instrument designed for the protection of the dual system, can liberty be impaired?

What a majestic procession of the canons of liberty are the amendments to the Constitution of the United States, adopted by the Fathers for the virtual preservation of the rights of the State. They are practically the principles for which men who have loved liberty and revered the ideals of patriotism in all times and in all countries have shed their blood and given their lives.

Listen to the enunciation of these great principles :

Congress shall make no law respecting an establishment of religion or abridging the freedom of speech or of the press, or the right of the people peaceably to assemble to petition the government for a redress of grievances. That the guarantees reserved to the States may not be valueless because they are without power, the right of the people to bear arms and maintain a well regulated militia for the security of the State shall not be infringed upon. The people shall be secure in their persons, houses, papers, and effects against unreasonable searches and seizures, and no warrants shall issue but upon probable cause supported by oath or affirmation describing the place to be searched and the person or thing to be seized. No person shall be held to answer for a capital or infamous crime unless on presentment or indictment of a grand jury, nor shall any person be subjected for the same offence to be twice put in jeopardy for life or limb, nor be compelled to be a witness against himself nor be deprived of life, liberty, and property without due process of law. Nor shall private property be taken for public use without just compensation. The accused shall enjoy the right to a speedy, public trial by an impartial jury of the vicinage, and he shall be informed of the nature and cause of the accusation and be confronted with the witnesses against him.   The right of trial by jury shall be jealously preserved, and excessive bail shall not be required or excessive fines imposed or unusual punishments inflicted. The judicial power of the United States shall not be construed to extend to any suit prosecuted against one of the United States by citizens of another or of a foreign state; and further, this precious heritage of liberty enunciates with distinctness and exactness the great cardinal principle of those who believe in the preservation of all the powers of the States in their absolute entirety and vigor, that the enumeration in the Constitution of certain rights shall not be construed to deny or disparage others retained by the people, and that the powers not delegated to the United States by the Constitution, nor prohibited by it to the States, are reserved to the States respectively or to the people.

The Fathers, touching hands with despotism, knowing the terrors of absolutism, having experience of unequal and unjust government, appreciating from war and wasted country and sacrifice that liberty could only be made permanent by the preservation of these great principles in the government which they were creating, gave that government to us hedged about with these precious principles which with undying vigilance and jealousy should be guarded.

How stand the governmental forces to-day? Have the great controlling canons of the country's life been preserved? Are the rights intended to be protected by those organic principles still intact?

Whilst the intention of the Fathers was so clear, their fear of a great central power so express, and their determination that the General Government should possess only the powers delegated to it, still every one who loves his country, whose eyes are not closed to its dangers, cannot but see that the powers of the General Government in every department of its life have infinitely broadened with the passing years. It is as plain that the rights and the powers of the State have been as surely narrowed. These tendencies have not been sporadic. Both tendencies have been equally continuous, steady, and sure. By interpretation and explanation of the Constitution by the Supreme Court, by amendment as provided by the Constitution, by war, by congressional act, which is practically the expression of public opinion, the powers of the General Government have gathered strength, mighty and unprecedented, in the history of government. On the other hand is the significant fact that not one of the powers of the State have been widened by any influence, whether judicial decision, legislation, public opinion, war, or amendment. It is too plain to conceal that there has grown a feeling which would obliterate the rights of the State, which would invest in the strong hands of the General Government all of the powers which the Fathers believed were necessary to the State to keep free and perpetual the government which they had created. Within the last decade the vast material increase in the country's power and wealth and the widening of its horizon, governmental and commercial, seem to have swept away the great constitutional landmarks which have made possible the most marvellous development of liberty the world has ever seen.

A great Senator lately declared that with the growth of the country, the preservation of property, its management and control, is the chief interest of a great people.

Another authority, with the prestige of great place, declares that the condition of the day demands that theories of government should not be the subject of the people's contemplation but rather the administration of affairs.

A citizen of national repute voices the sentiment that commerce and development should know no State lines.

The infringement of fundamental laws is insidious, yet we have heard it boldly declared from the high place once occupied by Washington that : " In some cases this governmental action must be exercised by the several States individually. In yet others it has become increasingly evident that no efficient State action is possible, and that we need, through executive action, through legislation, and through judicial interpretation and construction of law, to increase the power of the Federal Government. If we fail thus to increase it, we show our impotence."

We have heard but yesterday from the great place

of the Secretary of State: " It may be that such control would better be exercised in particular instances by the government of the States, but the people will have the control they need either from the States or from the National Government, and if the State fails to furnish it in due measure, sooner or later constructions of the Constitution will be found to vest the power where it will be exercised — in the National Government."

These are but illustrations of the direction of public thought, that great constitutional limitations, which the fathers of free government thought vital, are not to be considered when they interfere in any manner with the interest or the feeling of the day. The exigencies of this occasion will only allow me to succinctly advert to them to show how marvellously swift has been the increase of the powers of the General Government and how equally sure has been the destruction of the rights of the States. It would surely be more pleasant to discuss the great principles involved in this subject, but the advance against the constitutional limitations of our country will be more readily appreciated by concrete illustration.

The Supreme Court, under the guidance of Chief Justice Marshall, whose name we speak with reverence, fearing a repetition of the experience under the original confederation of the States, steadily and quickly, by interpretation of the Constitution, widened and deepened the powers of the General Government. For thirty-five years during the formative period of our country's life the powers of the greatest English-speaking judge were directed to building, strong and secure, its foundations. A brief reference to the great principles decided shows that from the very beginning of the life of this co-ordinate branch of our government the fullest and broadest amplitude of interpretation and deduction of the Constitution has characterized the judgments of the Court.

" Let the end be legitimate, let it be within the scope of the Constitution, and all means which are proper, which are plainly adapted to that end, which are not prohibited, but consist with the letter and spirit of the Constitution, are constitutional," forms the broad judicial basis for the far-reaching corollaries and deductions around which has been built up the vast and steadily increasing power of the Federal Government.

How full are the years of the Court with the establishment of the great national powers of the government. How quickly is the direction towards the narrowing of the constitutional rights of the State. With the early years was the decision of the Supreme Court as to the establishment of the national bank and of the great principle forbidding the States to interfere with any of the constitutional methods of carrying out its provisions by the General Government. And quickly came the settlement of the supreme position of the Court for decision upon the Constitution, and the settlement of its own position as one of the great co-ordinate departments of the government, and with it the declaration of the supremacy of the Constitution.

Before the white sails of the ships had been furled by the power of steam came the establishment by judicial authority of the power of the General Government over interstate commerce and the practical and absolute control by the General Government of the navigable streams of the country, and with this enormous power quickly came the decision of this august tribunal giving to Congress the fullest amplitude and discretion in choosing the means to carry into effect the powers vested in the National Government, and giving the Supreme Court supervisory powers over the courts of the States. With these great powers was the decision that no State should annul a decision of the Federal Court, and the right to hold that a State law was unconstitutional, and that the Supreme Court was supreme as to the validity of a treaty. These are but mere mention of decisions in a direction which has never varied its steady course.

The determination of the machinery of government, as set out in the Constitution, was necessarily brief, but those administrative powers have been declared operative and effective by the widest judicial deduction.

From the taxing and borrowing and general welfare clauses of the Constitution, with the decisions of the Court denying the right of the States to interfere by taxation or otherwise, has grown all of the vast machinery as to tariffs and custom houses and national banks, and with the amplification of these powers the upholding of the

vast and complicated system of commercial law and of
civil provisions to carry into effect the powers but mentioned in the Constitution.   From the brief commerce
clause of the Constitution by the broad interpretation
and deduction as to its incidental powers by the Court
has grown the powerful machinery of administrative
law concerning transportation, immigration, improvement of rivers, building of harbors, control of commerce
between the States and foreign countries, and the authority to create railroad commissions with enormous
and increasing powers as to control of rates and
transportation.

Whilst such was the steady and sure trend of the
decisions of the Court, broadening and widening the
powers of the Federal Government, up to the great conflict between the States, since that time, by reason of
the post-bellum amendments, the rights of the National
Government have again been judicially broadened and
the rights of the States have been proportionally
narrowed.

We bow with reverence to the wisdom of the Fathers
in establishing a tribunal which protects the people
against themselves, for without it, in the fierce aftermath
of the war, amidst the feelings stirred by that great
conflict, the domestic and local rights of the State under a constitution subject to legislation, as is the British
constitution, would long since have perished, and we
would, whilst living under the forms of a republic, yet
be under the control of a consolidated government.

Says Justice Brewer, one of the great lawyers in the history of the Court, as to the decisions on the later amendments :

"While it may be said that the decisions thus far have been in restraint of the transfer by virtue of these amendments of the entire sovereignty of the State, yet the amendments themselves increase the power of the nation and give it a larger control over the internal life of the Republic, and to this extent tend to increase the one at the expense of the other. It must not be supposed that during this second period there has been any lessening on the part of the Supreme Court of a vigorous assertion of national stability. On the contrary, the ruling made in the first period has been re-affirmed and added to. And in upholding the provisions of the recent amendments, it has necessarily given a wider reach and an increased efficiency to the powers of the national government."

The decisions of the Court concerning the rights of the States under the Thirteenth, Fourteenth, and Fifteenth Amendments have increased the power of the General Government far beyond that ever contemplated by the Fathers. The decisions since the war have crowned with approval the exercise of sovereign powers never supposed to be inherent in the Constitution. In the Legal Tender Cases was the settlement of power beyond any ever before claimed for the General Government, that the National Government had been established with inherent sovereign powers, that the right to issue money in paper was therefore properly deduced from the constitutional right to coin and borrow money. A right so enormous in its reach and so revolutionary as to the basic powers of this government is beyond the conception of those who believe that this is a government of enumerated powers and that it can only exercise those expressly conferred upon it by the Constitution.

It ill becomes us to criticise the decisions of the great Court established by the Constitution, but when that Court decides that sovereign powers are inherent, every man who loves his country fears for the Constitution and the liberties of the people.

So in the Mormon Church Cases, the decision of the Court that the treaty-making power and the power to declare war gives the right to acquire territory, which power is incident to national sovereignty by reason of this power, the Court held that Congress had a right to legislate for this territory and had complete authority over its people and it was under its legislative discretion, and the National Government confiscated the property of the Church and diverted its proceeds to the general use.

Says a great lawyer :

" This decision became of extraordinary interest in connection with the extension of the jurisdiction of the United States over Porto Rico, Hawaii, and the Philippines, in 1898. If the construction of the Constitution which this decision made is to regulate the government of these new acquisitions, then the American people,

acting through Congress, can forbid the people of any
of these new acquisitions to assemble for the purpose
of political discussion, to petition our government for
redress of grievances, and to bear arms. Congress can
provide for searches and seizures of the persons dwelling in these acquisitions,—their houses, papers, and
effects,—in modes that are recognized as illegal when
employed in any American commonwealth.''

Such is the significance of the decision in the Insu-
lar Cases, which places outlying territory acquired by
treaty or war under a government such as Congress
may determine, in its discretion, whether different or
not from the government of other territories created
under the law of the land.

Under these latter decisions the great fundamental
right of trial by jury bequeathed to us by the common
law and guaranteed to us by the Constitution of the
Fathers has been abrogated in the colonies and dependencies owned by the United States, and life may be
taken by judicial process and the victim may walk to
the scaffold or suffer loss of liberty or property without
ever having looked upon the faces of the twelve jurymen who for a thousand years, under fundamental law,
have stood between those living under Anglo-Saxon
institutions and the loss of life, liberty, and property.

This discussion, necessarily brief, has been made to
illustrate the tremendous significance of the fact that
from the institution of the Supreme Court down to the
present day, the whole trend of its decisions has been

to the upholding and strengthening of the powers of the National Government and relatively depleting and destroying those of the States and the people.

It is adverted to furthermore to show that its latter decisions have grasped strange ideas of power which if carried to the ultimate conclusion will surely and absolutely break down the constitutional guarantees of the State and impair the liberty of the people.

Whilst in the judicial department we have witnessed this gradual and sure increase in the power of the National Government, it is in the administrative, executive, and legislative branches of our government where its advance has been most appalling. The Fathers feared a paternal government. A paternal government was the government with which they were acquainted in history and experience. They provided expressly through the amendments that the "enumeration in the Constitution of certain rights shall not be construed to deny or disparage others retained by the people," and further "the powers not delegated to the United States by the Constitution, nor prohibited by it to the States, are reserved to the States respectively or to the people."

Yet, notwithstanding these express provisions, the General Government, by legislation, administrative or executive action, or judicial decision, has invaded many reserved rights of the States and the people. Is not this never-ceasing tendency one to excite the fear of those who love our country? Should not patriotism be alarmed? Should not this governmental direction be arrested? Will not some day the usurper come? Should not patriotism grasp the weapon presented by the Fathers, and demand the preservation of the State with all of its powers? In what part of our land shall the battle-cry for the protection of the constitutional rights of the people and of the State be more resolutely heard than from this old University, redolent with blood shed for liberty, whose whole life is glorified by patriotic effort, and whose sons in every war of our country have laid aside the book and grasped the sword?

Where more sacred soil to speak of love of country! Where more hallowed fane, on bended knee to pray for guidance! To what temple do more thronging memories of loving sacrifice for country cling like the lichens and mosses of time than to these venerable walls! Christened at thy birth with the very name of liberty, glorified with the thought and regard of the Father of our Country, hallowed with the gentleness and the love of him who was part of our sacrifice, we reverence thee for what thou hast done. Where in all of this broad land of lake and river and fertile field such inspiration for liberty and holy love of country! I would call on thy sons from Yorktown and King's Mountain and Valley Forge, from New Orleans, from Chapultepec and Vera Cruz, from Gettysburg, Antietam, Port Republic, and Appomattox, and pray that their exaltation of love of country, supreme to all thought of life or earthly care, would descend upon thy children to-day assembled in this thy holy place.

Guarded by the spectral hosts of thy sons, "all the knees of which have not bowed unto Baal and every mouth which hath not kissed him," may thy power, partaking of the life of thy encircling mountains, on whose altars the beacon fires of liberty in every crisis of our country have flamed wide and clear, inspire for great and holy things those who walk under the watch and ward of thy towers. May peace linger around thy walls, from whose wide portals no one was ever turned, although clothed in the sackcloth of poverty, and whose broad democracy demands only integrity and character as the supreme requisites for thy sons.

The sections of the Constitution defining congressional power to lay and collect taxes, to provide for the common defence and general welfare of the United States, to coin and borrow money, to regulate commerce with foreign nations and among the several States, to establish post-roads and post-offices, and with the right to make laws necessary and proper for carrying into execution these constitutional powers, have been the forces invoked for legislative and administrative advance and for power to curtail and abrogate the rights of the people and of the State. There is only time for a brief mention of the most startling exercises of the Federal advance. To discuss executive encroachment will hurry this address into the forbidden domain of politics.   Hence I will advert only to some phases of Congressional usurpation.

Under the interstate commerce power which was practically intended by the founders of the government to prevent the States from placing charges upon interstate commerce, which commerce practically meant water transportation from the rivers and harbors of the different States, there has grown an enormous and increasing control of the domestic government of the States, which was never contemplated by the Fathers. The charges contemplated were the charges placed upon commerce by the exaction of a harbor license or other local tax by one State upon the commerce coming in from or going out to another.   Yet under these powers, which were relatively slight, has grown the inordinate control of interstate commerce.

Under the later constructions of this clause, practically nothing which grows from the ground, nothing concerning the morals of the people, nothing which touches our commercial life and which we eat or wear, is excepted from its all-consuming power.   To glorify its demands for control of all commerce our hallowed guarantees are threatened and the rights of the States are held for naught.   Amplifying the enormous power of the Interstate Act, Congress has passed the act providing for the control by the General Government of foods and drugs in interstate commerce.   This means that under the power of this law every product of food or drink, every drug or substance which could be used to sustain life, whether pure or not, is under the control, inspection, management, and transportation of the Federal Government. Thus the domestic and police laws of the State, in so far as they touch these great products necessary to life, are destroyed and placed under the control of the ever-widening powers of the Federal Government.

This omnipotent clause has not alone grasped the foods of the people, their labor, and their drink, but it has taken cognizance and control of their morals. In the effort to do away with the effect of lotteries, which in itself all will commend, the powers of the act were invoked and under its provisions a lottery ticket was decided to be a subject of commerce and its carriage was held to be against the Interstate Commerce Act and thus the lottery was destroyed. This decision was for the purpose alone of reaching a moral question. Interstate commerce was a mere pretence. Such is the effect of the law passed to prevent and forbid the manufacture of oleomargarine. This was under the taxing clause of the Constitution, and was for the frankly avowed purpose of destroying the manufacture of oleomargarine and protecting another industry. The bill became a law notwithstanding the avowal of its sponsors that its purpose was, through the governmental power of taxation, to destroy the manufacture of oleomargarine, and that the passage of the law would not produce a dollar of revenue to the government, and we have here one of the great powers of the Federal Government used for a purpose entirely different from that contemplated by the law under which the bill was passed.   However important and commendable the purpose, is it not dangerous beyond words when the tremendous powers of the Federal Government are invoked for one purpose when another purpose is actually sought to be effected?   What can we expect?   Powers which are sought to-day for a good purpose may be sought for an improper purpose to-morrow.   This government is a government of limited powers.   Our fathers feared a government of unlimited powers.   They placed restrictions around every act of the General Government and if those restrictions are to be removed for one purpose, is not the precedent afforded for these enormous powers being used for sinister purposes against the life of the State and the liberties of the people?   Says a great lawyer and writer:

" This lottery case is the most important, as bearing upon the relations between our state and national governments and the powers vested in each, which ever has been decided by the United States Supreme Court. If it is to remain the law, the idea of the founders that the power vested in Congress was simply to protect commerce from acts of interference by state governments has been wholly destroyed.   The right of the national government to pass a pure food law, or a prohibitive tax on oleomargarine, an act to prevent the importation of teas below a certain quality or flavor, and proposed laws for the regulation of insurance and hours of labor in various employments, are all dependent upon the soundness of this decision. Can it be that the power given Congress to regulate commerce between the states was intended to permit it to enter upon the reformation of society?"

Under this decision Congress may place upon interstate commerce any restrictions it may wish. When will this power find its limitations?— for, says the Court in this case:

"The present case does not require the court to declare the full extent of the power that Congress may exercise in the regulation of commerce among the states."

Pardon further concrete illustrations of the expansion of the governmental powers under the Interstate Act at the expense of the rights of the States and the people. A license is demanded in high places for the control of goods sent from one State to another. Under this theory of government may we not soon see every engineer and fireman of a train carrying commodities between States, every clerk who signs a bill of lading or check for interstate commerce, and every workman who trundles a cart laden with the goods of interstate commerce compelled to have a license, and look to the General Government as the representative of his life, labor, and protection? To-day every engineer, fireman, or telegraph operator employed in interstate commerce has his hours of labor and method of employment regulated by congressional act. The Senate of the

United States has just rested from the conflict over the introduction of the law and its advocacy by a distinguished Senator, placing child labor through this power under the control of the General Government and regulating its hours of labor and the age and conditions of its employment. Shall we not soon see all labor under governmental control?

Under the influence of this act eighty per cent. of the coal, the cotton, the wheat, the corn, the ore, and the other vast and unnumbered products of the ground and labor are practically under the control of the General Government. With the continual and steady lengtheuing and the broadening of the powers of this act it is difficult to know where and when the wheat of the farmers, the coal of the miners, the cotton of the planter comes under the jurisdiction of the Federal Government.

In none of the departments of the great paternal and despotic governments of the world is there a greater exercise of paternalism than is witnessed in the Department of Agriculture. In this Department is the greatest assault upon the rights of the State in the history of this government. In the midst of the waving corn and the golden wheat, beside the running water, and under the blue sky and the bright sun, surrounded by the fruits and the flowers which the power of independent labor has brought into blessed life, we have been taught is to be found the purest and most unselfish patriotism. This citadel of patriotism has been invaded. Without one line of constitutional power, against the express statement of the Fathers in convention assembled, in the institution of this government, this Department has been created and it has usurped the most sacred rights of the State. It has practically assumed control of the domestic life of the country. It is expending millions teaching the people what to eat. It has invaded the kitchen, telling the housewife how to cook. It is showing the farmers how to feed and raise stock. It is telling the people what to drink and wear. It is analyzing and testing foods and giving the farmers seed to sow and telling them how to reap. It is destroying bugs and worms. It is building roads. It is planting and distributing seeds and flowers and plants and vines and trees. It is testing ploughs and reapers and thrashers. It is raising stock. It is invading the homes of the farmers and showing them, through teachers' and farmers' institutes, how to till the land. It is experimenting upon the raising of horses and sheep and hogs and cattle. It is raising camels and operating ostrich farms. It is working plantations, upon which is raised everything which is eaten or worn or drunk by man. It is teaching schools. It is raising tea. Its vast and varied ramifications have invaded every province of the State. It has spent millions upon irrigation and is arranging to sell water upon a scale which minimizes the Egyptian government supplied by all the waters of the Nile. Under the provisions of this Department millions are appropriated to State normal schools, mechanical schools, agricultural schools, and high schools, thus making the most insidious attack upon the very heart of State life, and all of this without one line in the Constitution giving it any power whatsoever. With these enormous powers so lately assumed and in full growth, how soon will it be before the General Government will further invade the remaining rights of the State and take charge of the schools of the land? It has the power to do so if it has the power it is at present exercising. A bill is pending in Congress and is being pushed by powerful influences, providing for appropriation to the State schools and providing for certain governmental supervision over them. Only a few years ago one of the great contests in this country was to prevent the government from practically assuming control of the schools of the State. When the General Government educates the citizen the character of the Republic has been undermined to its very foundation. Under this sentiment, looking towards governmental authority and control, the militia of the country, by the National Militia Act, has been placed in close connection with, and under the supervision of, government officers. This bill especially provides for the acting together of the State militia and the troops of the government, and for the teaching of the State officers by the General Government, and provides for their subsistence whilst so engaged. Framers of the Constitution feared a standing army under the influence of the government. They solemnly provided for the right of the States to bear arms and for the separate State life of the militia.

Whilst in every department of the General Government we witness the disregard of the States' rights and the infringement of constitutional powers and the gradual control of the affairs of the people by the General Government, yet the growth of this sentiment in civil life, in commercial affairs and public sentiment is most marked. Time will allow me the mention of but few instances of this marvellous change in public sentiment as to governmental control and its effect. This new spirit has permeated every part of our life. Under the miasma of this fell influence, which looks only to convenience and success, gathering its volume from the busy toil of millions of men, has grown the feeling that congressional action is the proper course to control every demand and supply every deficiency in the life of the people. Under this influence a great convention, forgetting the sacredness of settled law, despising the landmarks between unlimited power and constitutional right, solemnly declares that the coal mines should be under the control of the General Government. This spirit demands governmental ownership of railroads and asks that the General Government guarantee the deposits of national banks. It is demanding a bureau to take practical control of the mining of coal. It asks for control of divorce. It seeks supervision of all corporations. Congressional

action and governmental control is the panacea for all
ills and is the hope of every interest. It has affected
the very life of the State governments and the State
courts. The powers of the State under the Constitution
are as supreme within its sphere as are the powers of
the General Government within its sphere. For the
great purpose for which they were created the powers
of the State are absolutely complete and effective. The
justice of the peace under the State is as full of effective
power within the State jurisdiction as is the United
States commissioner. The sheriff of the county in
one form or another has been enforcing the law, serving
the writs, preserving the peace under the civil life of
the Anglo-Saxon for a thousand years. The great inter-
mediate *nisi prius* courts of the State are as full of jurisdiction within the State, in every matter coming before
them, as are the District and Circuit Courts of the
United States. Yet in the great crises who appeals to
these representatives of the powers of the State? In
every case they are clothed with full and complete
power. In every case they have the full military and
civil power of the State to enable them to carry out
their orders and decrees. In no case within our experience has this power which can be summoned by
the officers of the State proved insufficient when there
was vigor and courage and character in the action of
the State officials. Notwithstanding this plenitude
of State power every excuse is sought to appeal to the
jurisdiction and officials of the National Government.

In a great social cataclysm, with lawlessness unloosed, with thousands of men threatening the peace of the State, with full desire and ability on my part to preserve its rights, with a successful and earnest effort being made to do so, my contest was not alone with the powers of lawlessness, but also with those who were clamoring for the interference and control of the United States Government.

I have already transgressed too severely upon your patience for further illustration of this change of sentiment as to the exercise of the functions of our governmental life.

The Fathers intended that this great dual system should be preserved in its entirety. Thus they created it and so they intended it to live. They gave it to us blessed with their patriotic endeavor, and it is a heritage from those who believed that the correct application of its co-equal powers was vital to the life of the Republic. Pursuing the course that we are following to-day the result is inevitable. The great lines of constitutional demarcation between the State and the General Government will be destroyed. If the General Government, contrary to the spirit and letter of the Constitution, exercises rights which have no place among its limited and delegated powers, the Constitution will rapidly become an instrument which public opinion may change to suit its interests and the convenience of the day, conforming to the dictum of a late Vice-President of the United States that "its most remarkable feature is its

elastic flexibility, and its latent power through which
it has been enabled to conform to the necessities, the
passions, and the aspirations of the people.'' If these
strange doctrines are allowed to pervade the life of the
people as to the theories and rights of government, efficiency of action, power in execution and splendor of
accomplishment will be looked to as the object of government and as superior to the care and preservation of
the sacred rights which have come down to us from the
Fathers. And let me enter my protest against the
proposition that we are pessimists, who demand that
this government shall be administered in the spirit in
which it was bequeathed to us and that the Constitution
shall be adhered to in the substance and the letter.
We, who believe that reserved rights should not be invaded, that delegated powers shall not become sovereign
and despotic are not pessimists. No patriot would arrest the advancing life of the country. We appreciate
that the progress of the day needs broad and liberal
policies, but these policies of progress do not demand
that we for them should destroy constitutional rights.
We understand that this great Republic with its wealth
of production demands the world for its market, but no
triumph of material life will atone for a broken Constitution. We well know that vigorous action in the great
matters of the day is necessary, but that vigor of execution does not require that the basic and historic principles of a free people should be destroyed. We do not
believe in the narrow and impracticable interpretation

of the Constitution which would destroy its efficiency. We believe that the Constitution should be interpreted in the broadest spirit and on the fairest lines, but that its construction should not be wrenched nor its powers broadened beyond the thought of those who created this wonderful instrument. We believe that Congress may exercise all the powers that are plainly incidental to, deducible from, and not prohibited by the Constitution. We believe that the executive officers of the General Government should use that marvellous instrument for the purposes for which it was established and no further. We believe that if the exigencies of modern life demand the amendment of the Constitution, that it shall be amended, not by act of Congress, sentiment of the people, or judicial construction, but that it shall be amended as provided in the Constitution. We demand no narrow construing of its provisions. We only ask an honest construction of the Constitution, and demand that the vast rights of the General Government, already sufficiently strong for all the purposes for which they were intended, shall not be by implication unfairly extended, nor by usurpation misused.

How shall the sentiment of the day be directed to the ways so long trod by us in safety and contentment? Reverence for the hallowed traditions surrounding the birth of our country's life or an appeal to the naked words of the constitutional guarantees of the State will not preserve the equilibrium between the State and the

National Government, nor will mere jealousy of the growing ascendency of the National Government prevent it using powers not conferred. If we desire to maintain those rights it cannot be accomplished by a mere academic discussion of them. Patriotism demands infinitely more. The State must be exalted by its citizens, in its political, material, and moral life. The pride of the State in the maintainance of its powers must be revived. The character of the officials chosen by the State must be elevated. They must be taught by an enlightened and jealous public, that the rights of the State are sacred, and that he who through apathy or pusillanimity will allow any infraction of these rights will be Anathema. Am I not correct in asserting that under the spirit of the day the supreme object of patriotism should be the preservation of these great powers?

Only can we retain the constitutional position guaranteed to the State by holding strong and true its great rights. Let us reason plainly with each other as brothers, united in a patriotic cause. This is not the spirit which in many States of the Union has characterized those who have been entrusted with the conservation of the high powers of the State. We well understand that the widening sweep of the national life has never rested in its march of encroachment, yet this has not alone arisen from a desire of increased power by the National Government, but often because the rights of the State have not been upheld by its guardians. These rights have withered from the neglect of the States themselves. These rights have become quiescent through apathy. Sacred principles which uphold this marvellous fabric of our dual life have been supinely surrendered by those who controlled the destinies of the State. Governors to escape responsibility have allowed unconstitutional encroachment on States' rights for which they should have been impeached. Judges have allowed their jurisdiction to be invaded, for the permission of which the ermine should have been stripped from their shoulders. Legislators have allowed infractions of their constitutional powers, for which they should have been discredited and displaced by an outraged State. These conditions oftentimes prevailing have not always been due to those whom the State has elected to control its affairs. The officials of the State have not always been buttressed by a high State pride in the people, a love of constitutional right, an exalted patriotism which would command them to hold to the full for every right and dignity of the State. This revival of the high ideals of the State in the minds of its officials and citizens, this jealousy of the preservation of the sacred powers of the State by its guardians, can only be effected by the revival of supreme and exalted patriotism and reverence for the Constitution in the souls of the citizens of the country. This spirit should teach that the powers of the State, whether judicial, legislative, or executive, are equal in dignity, character, and importance to those of the National Government. This State spirit must live in the high character and fearless assertion of State life and in the insistent demand of the citizen that con- stitutional guarantees shall remain unbroken and un- impaired in the letter and in the spirit. The State cannot become a silent partner in this government. Its powers must be made vital and its rights effective, and its assertion of those great powers must be sustained by the feeling which holds patriotism the chiefest and loftiest sentiment of human life.

This crisis of our country demands, as never before, for its corrective, the vigorous life of the local ideal of patriotism. In this day of trial we appeal to the pristine unit of patriotism, the State, holding its chief power in the South no longer naked and powerless, but under Divine blessing thrilling with life and energy, and supported by a wealth of material power never surpassed by Imperial Rome or Old England. The South's material power, even in this day of mighty accomplishment and feeling, can dignify any sentiment and give potency to any demand for a return to the faiths of the Fathers. Its credit is restored, great cities, the seats of vast commerce in every part of our Southern land, are glowing with energy unsurpassed. The fertile fields are laughing with the perennial harvests growing into fatness under our sunny skies, and the waving grain bows its heavy head under the benediction of plenty. Great systems of railways are in tremendous struggle that they may be touched with the gleam of our golden lamp. Our mighty forests are

ringing with the sound of the saw and the axe, and our
towns echo with the joy of contented labor, and are
bright with the laughter of children at their play.   The
world is clothed with our cotton, and our towns are
alive with the whir of the spindles.   The red gleam of
the manufactories marks on our sky the figures of our
amazing wealth.   From our shipyards and deep harbors
the ships go on their trackless way, carrying our treasures to all peoples of the earth.   Over rivers and
through mountains and across the valleys thunders the
locomotive, living emblem of the vitality of our Southern
life.   From our mines pour uncounted millions of the
diamonds of commerce.   From the inexhaustible plenty
of the Creator stream rivers of oil.   By Southern sea
and broad river the trip-hammer beats a steady halle-
lujah of praise.   The machinery of our countless mills
never ceases its song of rejoicing.   Southern life is
no longer wrapped with cerements of mourning, but
crowned and glorified with the lilies and roses of prosperity and contentment.   When we contemplate her material wealth there arises before us the broad empire of
Rome; and we hear the rhythm of the oars of the trireme
as it ploughs its way over river and sea, laden with its
burden from the rich corn lands of Illyricum and Sicily
and Africa.   That fair temple and pillar may crown Imperial Rome, we hear the stroke of the whip, as sweat-
ing slaves quarry the marble from Pentelicus and
Numidia, from Arabia and Paros.   That Rome may
enslave the world, we see the inexorable taskmaster

fashioning sword and shackle in the red forges of Britain and Germany and Spain and Italy and Gaul. That ruby and sapphire may gleam in fillet and girdle, and that bread and the games be not denied the people, over the sands of the East hastens the dust-enshrouded caravan. For her, in Greece and Palestine and Asia Minor, the soft winds ripened the olive, and the pomegranate robbed the sun of its gold. For Rome, the cedars of Lebanon bowed their mighty heads, and Gaul and Britain gave of their oaks and their pines. That her altars might smoke with unfailing sacrifice and her phalanxes of iron and blood be strong, the shepherds watched with the stars on the plains of Esdraelon, and amidst the dews of the Elbe. When her iron legions had thundered past that she might pen her decrees to strange peoples and to far-off lands, through the soft waters of the Nile the papyrus lifted its slender stalk. That from Brundisia and Ostia the galleys filled with the legions could cover the sea from Phœnicia to the Pillars of Hercules, so that Rome might hold her tribute world and keep her iron hand on all the people, the Mediterranean slept in beauty and peace.

Here in our South are conditions of dominion beyond dreams of Roman consul or emperor. With ten millions more people than composed the Roman citizenship, with five hundred millions more of the inhabitants of the earth needing the products of our field and hand and workshop than were tributary to Imperial Rome, with more iron in one State than was in all of Britain and Spain and Gaul and Germany, with the ability to produce more bread ten times over than could Gaul and Africa and Sicily and the Nile, with more varied fruits in one State than could grow in all the fields and gardens of that kingdom of iron, never could Imperial Rome aspire to the real, material dominion easily within the grasp of the South. In our South, in one State, is sufficient marble to create again every temple and city which graced with glowing life the rivers and plains of the Imperial Kingdom. Here in the South are mighty rivers on whose bosoms float in one year argosies more precious than in one hundred years of Roman life vexed the current of the Tiber, the Seine, the Rhone, the Danube, and the Nile. Here, in the fields of one Southern State, grow the lowing herds, ample to supply every blood-stained altar of Rome with sacrifice and to furnish with food every Roman citizen. Here is everything needed for dominion, iron and gold, wine and oil, fruit and food, cotton and wool, tin and copper, timber and marble, in limitless quantities, yea, far beyond the voracity and capacity of Ancient Rome. Around this Southern land, He from whose urn poured the waters and whose hands fashioned the Continents has laid great oceans, and a mighty sea, from whose shores rise the majestic portals of the gateway to all the oceans and to all the people, a sea holding the land lovingly in deep embrace and whose smiling bosom is caressed by odor of fruit and flower and vine, from islands whose skies are brighter and whose soil is more life-giving than the magical lands of the Mediterranean.

Yea, more potent than Roman phalanx or the corn lands of Africa or the riches of the East, there walk with us the arts and sciences, and over our land, like the benison of a mother's blessing at eventide, fall the words of the Blessed Son of Man, "Thou shalt love thy neighbor as thyself."

Old England has placed her constitutional government, her customs, and her language, wherever woman loves and man can labor. Her hand is more potent in the directing of mankind's destinies than ever was that of Spanish king or Roman emperor. This material mastery she has achieved through her possession of iron and coal and through her ability to manufacture. One Southern State possesses more and better coal twice over, and the whole of the South has ten times more coal than England. One State of the South possesses more iron than the whole of mighty England, and without the South's cotton supply, the fires would die on the hearths of England's workmen and silence would reign in her busy streets.

Supported by a dignity of power dazzling even to the materialism of the day the South appeals to the Republic from a grander and a more exalted height than that of mere material power. From the depths of a patriotism which through conflict and sorrow has never lessened in its power, she asks the Republic to return to the old faiths and abide with us along the old ways of constitutional government.   Here in the South are the pristine ideals alive and virile.   Here is a homogeneous people, untouched by alien blood and holding hands through this native life with the Fathers of the Republic.

Amidst the thunderings and the lightnings of our day of trial the Tables of the Law were not broken. We have kept them unscathed by fire and unchanged by time, and holding them before the people ask that their sacred words be once more a guide to their feet wandering in far distant ways.   Dwelling under the lintels of the States which watched at the birth of the Republic, we are filled with a love of the olden ideals. With us has lingered those faiths and around the State has grown the sweetest and the most abiding sentiment and affection.   From race and tradition, and from sacrifice which appalled the world by the breadth of its unselfishness, there is with the South that wealth of local patriotism which jealously holds the State to its high and equal place in this government of co-ordinate powers.

Accepting the conclusions of the great conflict in the broadest and most catholic spirit, yet holding to the ancient principles of state government, with patriotism which knows no sectional feeling, we wish to hold up the hands of the Republic in this crisis of its civil life. With naught of feeling but love, we ask our brothers to dwell with us again under the same vine and tree and journey over the long-known road, and with us keep pure and untouched those great rights affecting with equal power the State and the Union.

The South would not for the wealth of the Indies destroy one power or impair one constitutional right of the Union. Its glorious life is the object of our pride and love, and its future the subject of our prayers. Love for the State is entirely consonant with affection for the Union. They should go hand in hand, neither seeking the powers, or desiring control of the rights of the other. The South believes that if in the crisis of our country's life the people grow towards "partial and transitory interests they would renounce the blessings prepared for them by the Revolution." The Fathers, with a wondrous prescience of the mighty power which would develop in the Republic, did not concern themselves with the protection of our country against foreign foes. They were more greatly interested as to our ability to exercise self-control within our internal life.

I have but endeavored to point out in the evolution of our country's life the evidences of the want of that self-control which is so necessary to a free people, and to indicate the great restraining influence against the radicalism which would destroy the ancient faiths. To you, young gentlemen, will be entrusted these great questions, with you will be the power for the years to come to decide the momentous problem, whether the Republic will go into the future a government of naked force filled with powers forbidden—or will you summon around you the spirits of the Fathers and pray for that exaltation of character which will preserve this Republic with its powers crowned with self-restraint, with its life blessed with holy and abiding patriotism, and its acts controlled by the high ideals which amidst sorrow and joy have been preserved as the dearest birthright of this blessed land of the South?

And may He who, for His own purpose, led our Fathers across the trackless sea to this goodly land, who blessed their labors with the night-tide and the morning sun, who in distress covered them with the deep shadow of His wing, lead you in these great matters to that conclusion which will lay no arresting hand on the progress of this people on its march for the uplifting of all of the nations of the earth.